Brassneck

Brassneck is a collaboration between two of the most talented of the young playwrights to emerge in Britain during the past five years, Howard Brenton and David Hare. First staged at the Nottingham Playhouse in September 1973, it tells the story of the rise and fall of the Bagley clan, in an imaginary Midlands town in post-war Britain. Spanning nearly thirty years, it shows three generations of Bagleys involved in a panoramic saga of local political in-fighting, social climbing and corruption.

'The play is marvellously quick-witted and exuberant – surprising perhaps, when you consider that it's all about the iniquity of capitalism.'

Benedict Nightingale in the *New Statesman*

'The production covers scenes of golf links, the hunting field and council offices, not to mention a lurid Vatican fantasy in which Alfred imagines himself crowned Pope . . . Altogether a triumphant evening.'

Irving Wardle in *The Times*

The photograph on the front cover shows Paul Dawkins in the Nottingham Playhouse production in September 1973, and is reproduced by courtesy of John Haynes. The photographs of David Hare and Howard Brenton on the back cover are reproduced by courtesy of Snoo Wilson.

BRASSNECK

Howard Brenton
&
David Hare

METHUEN · LONDON AND NEW YORK

A Methuen Paperback

*This edition first published in 1974 by Eyre Methuen Ltd
11 New Fetter Lane London EC4P 4EE
Reprinted 1985 by Methuen London Ltd
Published in the United States of America by
Methuen Inc., 733 Third Avenue, New York, NY 10017
Copyright © 1973 by Howard Brenton and David Hare
Printed in Great Britain by
Richard Clay (The Chaucer Press) Ltd, Bungay, Suffolk*

The extract from You Can't Always Get What You
Want *by Mick Jagger and Keith Richard is reproduced
by courtesy of Essex Music International Limited.*

ISBN 0 413 31760 9 (Paperback)

TO
Bill Gaskill

Brassneck was first presented at the Nottingham Playhouse on 19 September 1973 with the following cast:

ALFRED BAGLEY	Paul Dawkins
DRIVER	Tom Wilkinson
CLIVE AVON	Myles Hoyle
DUNCAN BASSETT	James Warrior
BILL ROCHESTER	Ralph Nossek
MR HARRINGTON	Roland Macleod
JAMES AVON	Griffith Jones
HARRY EDMUNDS	Bill Dean
JUNIOR DEACON	Tom Wilkinson
TOM BROWNE	Roger Sloman
CADDIES	Paul Kelly
	Eric Richard
CARDINALS	Tom Wilkinson
	Bob Hescott
HERMAPHRODITE	Paul Kelly
PORTER	Eric Richard
RODERICK BAGLEY	Jeremy Wilkin
SIDNEY BAGLEY	Jonathan Pryce
MARTIN BAGLEY	Colin Higgins
LUCY BAGLEY	Jane Wymark
VANESSA BAGLEY	Louise Breslin
PHOTOGRAPHER	Bob Hescott
MAJORDOMO	Tom Wilkinson
WAITER AT WEDDING	Bob Hescott
TAP DANCER	Liz Whiting
RAYMOND FINCH	Roland Macleod
FARMER'S BOY	Paul Kelly
FAN DANCER	Liz Whiting
STRIPPER	Brandy di Frank

Director	David Hare
Design	Patrick Robertson
Costumes	Rosemary Vercoe
Lighting	Rory Dempster
Associate Director	Richard Eyre

Authors' Note

Brassneck was written for the Nottingham Playhouse to coincide with Richard Eyre's appointment as Director there. It had a very fine cast. Projected scenery was used throughout. This solved many of the play's staging problems, and gave the documentary sequences between the scenes their proper weight.

In the writing, every scene, every word was jointly worked: there is nothing which is more one of us than the other. The work is indivisible.

'Brassneck' is a Midlands word meaning 'cheek' or 'nerve'. It has criminal connotations.

ACT ONE

SCENE ONE

A photograph of Churchill with the Royal Family on VE day as the audience comes into the theatre. Lights down. Photo fades.
A bare stage. At the roadside is an old man, ALFRED BAGLEY.
He carries a fine leather case. He looks weak, senile and slightly ill.
He is thumbing a lift.
A van drives on to the stage. It stops.

DRIVER. Where y'er off to, Da?
BAGLEY. Just . . . down there.
DRIVER. In ter Stanton? 'Op in then.
BAGLEY. I don't want a lift. I want a word with you. (*He staggers slightly and sits down on his case.*)
DRIVER. You a' right, Da?

    The DRIVER *gets down.*

DRIVER. Wor's a man o' yer age doin' on road?
BAGLEY. Made it from London.
DRIVER. Wha' thumbin'? Not a poor man, are yer?
BAGLEY. See England.
DRIVER. Yer daft.

    The DRIVER *gets some tea out from the cab, in a thermos.*

DRIVER. Tea?
BAGLEY. Thank you.

DRIVER. Then I'll drive yer down.

BAGLEY *sips his tea.*

BAGLEY. A fine prospect.

DRIVER. ?

BAGLEY. The town.

DRIVER. Bleddy hole. Born and bred.

BAGLEY. What's the big building with the dome?

DRIVER. Town 'All. Bleddy wonderful. All painted inside. Dome. Angels. Trumpets. All swirling. Bleddy marvellous.

BAGLEY. I had an angel once.

DRIVER. Oh yeah.

BAGLEY. On the mantelpiece. (BAGLEY *slops and dribbles his tea.*)

DRIVER. Yer all in. Get up in cab.

BAGLEY. How much do you want for the van?

DRIVER. Wha'?

BAGLEY. Thirty pounds?

DRIVER. I'll not take 'owt off yer for me van.

BAGLEY. Perhaps forty pounds. (*He gets the money out of the suitcase.*)

DRIVER. Jus' like tha'? Nice as pie?

BAGLEY. Forty-five pounds. I'll not go beyond forty-five.

DRIVER. Bleddy 'ell fire.

BAGLEY. Free country. Fair transaction.

DRIVER. That's bleddy silly. Forty-five pounds. (*He weakens.*) Want a bit o' money for wha' I got up back.

BAGLEY (*looking at the sign on the side of the van*). Milk powder?

Pause.

DRIVER. 'Appen it's silk.

BAGLEY. Silk.

Pause.

BAGLEY. Silk is rarely come by.

DRIVER. Oh aye.

BAGLEY. Unless it's Luftwaffe silk. German parachutes.

DRIVER. Yer know. RAF lads . . .

BAGLEY. People do not take kindly to Luftwaffe silk. We have not been through a war for nothing, young man. It will be extremely hard to find a retailer. Give you another fifteen for the load. That's sixty. Van and stock.

DRIVER. A' right. A' right.

BAGLEY. Agreed.

DRIVER. I thought yer were 'alf dead a moment ago.

BAGLEY. Done.

DRIVER. Don't yer wan' ter look silk over?

BAGLEY moves away.

BAGLEY. Pig in a poke. The van's what I want.

DRIVER. Oh aye.

The DRIVER gets his stuff out of the van.

DRIVER. I 'eard there were free food in London streets on VE day. Whole chickens roasted and given away. Did yer see tha'?

BAGLEY. I don't know. I didn't notice. I'd already decided to come North. (*They shake.*) Very pleasant to have met you. My card.

DRIVER. Oh aye.

BAGLEY gets into the van and drives off. The DRIVER looks at the card.

DRIVER. Alfred Bagley. (*Pause.*) Bagley.

Blackout.

SCENE TWO

Photographs. Election 1945. Churchill and Attlee. Polling booths. Election posters. Bevin, Cripps, the young Wilson. Front page of

*'Daily Mirror' announces Labour victory. Music. The 'Red Flag'
sung joyously. Lights up.*

AVON's *home.* BAGLEY *is alone in a huge hall. An argument offstage.
Then* CLIVE *enters, a fairhaired young man. Upper class manner.
He wears an RAF uniform and has a wounded foot.*

CLIVE. My father will see you in a moment. He's with a flock of
local Tory bigwigs. They're all a bit shirty. As you can imagine.
BAGLEY. Ah. Socialism. Yes. (*He points at* CLIVE's *foot.*)
Wounded?
CLIVE. 'Fraid so. Mine's just the ankle, but Dad's is up to here.
Something of a family tradition. To get it in the leg. (*He hits
his thigh.*) Swept into Berlin, but left his right leg floating down
the Rhine. Strange to think of a hunk of my father feeding the
fishes in the North Sea. A very brave man.
BAGLEY. And you?
CLIVE. Oh, nothing. Nothing. German night fighter, I'm afraid.
Had my foot in the wrong place. Never foxtrot in a Lancaster.
BAGLEY. Still, we won.
CLIVE. What? (*He looks at* BAGLEY.) Oh yes.

Enter JAMES AVON, *42, upright and genial.* BILL ROCHESTER,
30, thin, earnest, musty. DUNCAN BASSETT, *27, aggressive,
and* MR HARRINGTON, *55, strained and skullish.*

ROCHESTER (*off*). Duncan. Duncan.
BASSETT. A red flag fluttering over Town 'All dome . . .
HARRINGTON. Bravado.
BASSETT. It's still there. Been there eight hours.
ROCHESTER. You're not saying Edmunds put it up there himself.
BASSETT. Wouldn't put it past him. My father –
AVON. Please, gentlemen . . .
BASSETT. My father taught me that there is a class war. Which
you neglect at your peril. As a brewer he saw it every day.
AVON. Please . . .
BASSETT. Till he died.

AVON. Please. We agree. A delegation to Edmunds.

BASSETT. Just make him feel important.

AVON. He is important. Whatever our personal feelings he is our new MP.

ROCHESTER. I think if James tries his famous personal approach . . .

AVON. Certainly worked in the past.

BASSETT. That were when he were just Union leader in our brewery.

AVON. He was always most gentlemanly. Chummy.

BASSETT. Chum's puffed up now. Bloated with pride. Stanton's given 'im a majority as big as the eighth army.

ROCHESTER. If your brewery is nationalized, Duncan, you'll need Edmunds on your side to get proper compensation.

BASSETT. I'd let the lot gush out into public drains before I crawled to Harry Edmunds. It's a basic freedom. To brew your own ale in your own way.

CLIVE. Father, a Mr Bagley for you.

BASSETT. Freedom.

BAGLEY. I was told you were the estate agent in the town.

They all look at BAGLEY. *Pause.*

AVON. Welcome, my dear fellow. Pleasure to do business. Pleasure-to-do-business. Pleasure to welcome you into my home. You've met Clive. He's going to be an architect.

BAGLEY. Ah.

AVON. This is Mr Bassett. Mr Harrington. Rochester.

ROCHESTER (*smiles.*) Hello.

AVON. This is Mr . . .

CLIVE. Bagley.

AVON. Of course it is. We're all slightly over-excited at the election result, Mr Bagley.

BAGLEY. Ah.

AVON. We've got to live with it, gentlemen. Talk to Edmunds offer him friendship and good sense.

They start to go out.

BASSETT. Live with it? Live in it, more like. Soviet State.

AVON. Cheer up, Duncan.

ROCHESTER. Good bye for now, Mr Bagley.

BAGLEY. Yes.

BASSETT. Dear Lord God, and I thought I were coming back to England. England . . . (*They've gone.* AVON *turns to* BAGLEY.)

AVON. Ha. Mustn't delay. My first customer under the new regime. I hear when the Election result was declared, an empty taxi drew up outside 10 Downing Street, and Mr Attlee got out.

Pause.

CLIVE. My father wants me to leave before you fall to discussing business. (*He shakes* BAGLEY's *hand.*) Toodle oo. (*He goes out.*)

BAGLEY. Yes.

AVON. Pulls the carpet out, doesn't it. Here I am trying to earn a living and any moment they may nationalize the land.

BAGLEY. Oh, I don't think Attlee . . .

AVON. Well, at their last conference . . .

BAGLEY. No, I'm sure . . .

AVON. Hot air, you'd say?

BAGLEY *raises an eyebrow.*

Anyway. Can but do and die. How can I help?

BAGLEY. I'm looking for somewhere to live.

AVON. Fine.

BAGLEY. I'm very old. I'm looking for somewhere to die.

AVON. Ah. (*Caught on the wrong foot.*) Fine. Splendid.

BAGLEY. I come from this town.

AVON. Really?

BAGLEY. 1869.

AVON. Born?

BAGLEY. And now I want to return.

AVON. Well, I'm an estate agent. That's my job. (*Pause.*) A home then.

BAGLEY. Well, not a home exactly.

AVON. I see.

BAGLEY. More . . . Some homes. Some houses.

AVON. Ah. With you.

BAGLEY. Several houses. Many houses. Land. Property. Rows of houses. Back-to-backs and terraces. Anything. All the property I can buy. As many houses as we can find. (*Pause.*) Just so I have somewhere to die.

AVON. Feather the bed to lie on.

BAGLEY. . . . That.

AVON. I see. Yes. Very clearly where we are.

BAGLEY. Do you get . . . Much pain?

Pause.

AVON. Ah. (*He pats his leg.*) Freddy. We all had different kinds of Wars.

BAGLEY *takes an envelope from his pocket and unscrews a fountain pen.*

AVON. Eh . . .

BAGLEY *laboriously writes a figure on the envelope, then hands it to* AVON.

BAGLEY. I was going to say my capital would be . . .

AVON (*reading*). Oh yes.

BAGLEY. How many houses would I get for that, Mr Avon?

Pause.

AVON. Are you still in business, Mr Bagley?

BAGLEY. No, no, not at all.

AVON. I see.

BAGLEY. No longer. Hardly at all. I was a draper. I had two shops. Both went, very early on. My wife was killed. One of those . . . Funny little things in the Blitz.

AVON. Ah yes.

BAGLEY. She fell down the steps of an air-raid shelter. We all have stories to tell.

AVON. We all had different kinds of Wars . . .

BAGLEY. So it's all come to an end for me, in London. After I laid Angela to rest, I just had the compensation from the two shops and what I managed to put aside. And I wanted to come home to Stanton. (*He nods at the piece of paper.*) How far will it go, Mr Avon?

AVON. Houses? I think we could manage a good round . . . Three or four. At the modest end of the market, of course.

BAGLEY. I am prepared to go to the limit of my means. And quite impartially. I mean, I don't mind if they're slums.

AVON. In that case I'd say a round . . . Half dozen?

BAGLEY. Are Rochester and Rochester reliable solicitors?

AVON. Oh more, more than reliable. Trustworthy, even. That was Bill Rochester here just now.

BAGLEY. I know. I went to see him this morning. (*Pause.*) Said he'd put me up for the Conservative Club.

A long pause. BAGLEY *coughs twice.*

AVON. Come. Let me shake you by the hand. (*Pause.*) Shake you by the hand. (*He hasn't done it yet. Just repeats the phrase.*) I'm going to shake you now. By the hand. (*He shakes* BAGLEY's *hand.* BAGLEY *is mystified.*)

AVON. I'm shaking your hand.

BAGLEY. Yes.

AVON. I'm shaking it.

BAGLEY. Yes.

AVON. I wonder if . . . By the way, my name is James.

BAGLEY. Alfred.

AVON. I wonder, Alfred, if what you really want is not so much a house. As a lodge.

BAGLEY. Lodge?

AVON. Lodge.

BAGLEY. I want houses. Property. Any property at all. I've got a van, don't worry, for the rented property. To move furniture in. Or out.

AVON. Yes yes. (*Slowly.*) Now houses mean what? Architects. Builders.

BAGLEY. I'll have to go into the state of repair.

AVON. But we all need builders, don't we. All of us together. The whole of the business . . . Brotherhood . . . Need builders . . .

BAGLEY. . . . Yes . . .

AVON. What used to be called . . . Can you supply the word?

BAGLEY. Are you all right?

AVON. What?

BAGLEY. Is it the leg?

AVON. Listen. Men who work with stone. Who work with stone. Are you getting there? Another word, like builders.

BAGLEY. Blitzkrieg, is it? The old Blitzkrieg worrying you?

AVON. What are you talking about?

BAGLEY. What?

AVON. A word for bloody builders, man.

BAGLEY. Bricklayers?

AVON. Warm.

BAGLEY. Carpenters.

AVON. Warmer.

BAGLEY goes up to him and shakes his hand.

BAGLEY. Shake the hand. Is that what you want?

AVON. Shake the hand. Lay the stone. Build the temple. *Masons.*

BAGLEY. Masons.

A long pause.

AVON. It is a condition of membership of the Masonic Lodge that no man is asked to join. Each man must volunteer. The Masonic Order is a secret society. I have already gone too far in revealing myself. If you don't approach me soon, I shall be forced to leave the room.

Pause.

BAGLEY. I would like to volunteer to join the local Masonic Lodge.

   AVON *is cagey*.

AVON. Ah.

BAGLEY. Can you help?

AVON. I might be able to. I won't say yes and I won't say no.

   A pause. Then AVON *strides across the room, pleased.*

Shake you by the hand. Just the kind of chap we need. Happy with the town, keen to be happy *in* the town.

BAGLEY. I've got a load of parachute silk in a van outside. I was wondering if a reasonable price could be found. Perhaps a seventh house. I would be . . . Easier in my mind, with a seventh.

AVON. Yes yes. No trouble.

BAGLEY. About the houses . . .

AVON. Later. Later. That doesn't matter. On to the Lodge.

BAGLEY. The houses.

AVON. The Lodge.

   Blackout.

SCENE THREE

Photographs. Civic dignitaries at banquets. Opening fetes. Giving speeches. We get closer to them each time. Then the faces of the country's most famous Masons. Sixteen at a time. Then the legend: 'And one million other foursquare men.' Music: the hymn 'All people that on earth do dwell.'
Lights up.

A Masonic Lodge. Pillars, desks, ashlars etc. with globes, footstools, benches. Authentic.

On stage are HARRY EDMUNDS, BILL ROCHESTER, DUNCAN
BASSETT, JAMES AVON, *and* MR HARRINGTON. *Also three or
four other men. They are wearing dinner jackets with sashes and
aprons and fancy cuffs.*

At once from the back three loud knocks. DUNCAN BASSETT *takes
a short pace forward with the left foot and brings the right heel into
the instep to form a T. He then brings the outstretched thumb of the
right hand to the left of his windpipe, keeping the elbow horizontal
to the body.*

BASSETT. Brother Edmunds, there is a report.

   EDMUNDS *bangs his gavel and performs the same move.*

EDMUNDS. Brother Harrington, there is a report.
HARRINGTON. Brother Edmunds, enquire who wants admission.
EDMUNDS. Brother Bassett, see who wants admission. (BASSETT
   slits his throat and goes to the door. He opens it.)
BASSETT. Whom have you there?
CLIVE (*from outside*). Mr Alfred Bagley, a poor candidate in a
   state of darkness, who now comes of his own free will and
   accord, humbly soliciting to be admitted to the mysteries and
   privileges of Freemasonry.
HARRINGTON. Brother Deacons. Let him be admitted in due
   form.

   Through the door comes BAGLEY. *He is wearing a blindfold
   and a noose round his neck. His left breast is bared and his
   right sleeve above his elbow. His left trouser leg is up above his
   knee and on his right foot is a slipper. As he comes in* BASSETT
   pricks his bared breast with the point of a poniard.

ROCHESTER. Do you feel anything?
BAGLEY. Yes.

   The DEACONS *escort* BAGLEY *to a kneeling stool.*

HARRINGTON. Mr Alfred Bagley, I demand of you, are you a
   free man and of the full age of twenty-one years?

BAGLEY. I am.

HARRINGTON. Thus assured I will thank you to kneel while the blessing of Heaven is invoked on our proceedings.

> HARRINGTON *gives a single knock which is answered by* EDMUNDS *and* AVON. *All stand and place their right hands on their left breast. They cross wands over* BAGLEY's *head.*

HARRINGTON. In all cases of difficulty and danger, in whom do you put your trust?

BAGLEY. In God.

HARRINGTON. Right glad am I to find your faith so well founded, for where the name of God is invoked no danger can ensue.

> ROCHESTER *leads* BAGLEY *to the pedestal and directs him to stand with his heels together and his feet at right angles.*

EDMUNDS. Take a short pace with your left foot, bringing the heels together in the form of a square. Take another, a little longer, heel to heel as before. Another, still longer, heels together as before.

> BAGLEY *is now right in front of the pedestal.* ROCHESTER *stands on his left.*

HARRINGTON. You will now kneel on your left knee, your right foot formed in a square, give me your right hand, which I place on the Volume of the Sacred Law while your left will be employed in supporting these compasses, one point presented to your naked left breast.

> HARRINGTON *gives a single knock.* AVON *and* EDMUNDS *reply. Everyone puts their hands up to the slitting position and the two men cross wands over* BAGLEY's *head.*

Repeat your name at length and say with me: I, Alfred Bagley . . .

BAGLEY. I, Alfred William Ewart Bagley . . .

HARRINGTON { . . . in the presence of the great architect of
BAGLEY   { the Universe, of my own free will and
          { accord do hereby . . .

HARRINGTON *touches* BAGLEY'*s right hand with his left hand.*
. . . and hereon . . .

HARRINGTON *touches the Bible with his left hand.*

. . . sincerely and solemnly promise and swear that I will
always hele, conceal, and never reveal any part or parts, point
or points of the secrets or mysteries of, or belonging to, free
and accepted masons in masonry.

HARRINGTON { (*together*). I further solemnly promise that I
BAGLEY   { will not write these secrets, indite, carve,
          { mark, engrave or otherwise delineate them
          { on anything moveable or immoveable, under
          { the canopy of heaven. These several points
          { I solemnly swear to observe without evasion,
          { equivocation, or mental reservation of any
          { kind, under no less a penalty than that of
          { having my throat cut across . . .

BAGLEY *begins to lag behind.*

BAGLEY. Cut across . . .
HARRINGTON. My tongue torn out by the root . . .
BAGLEY. My tongue torn out by the root . . .
HARRINGTON. And buried in the sand of the sea at low water
  mark . . .
BAGLEY. Sand of sea low water mark . . .
HARRINGTON. Or a cable's length from the shore . . .
BAGLEY. Cable's length . . .
HARRINGTON. Where the tide regularly ebbs and flows twice in
  twenty-four hours . . .
BAGLEY. Flows . . .
HARRINGTON. Or the more effective punishment of being
  branded as a wilfully perjured individual, void of all moral

worth and totally unfit to be received into this worshipful
Lodge . . .

BAGLEY. So help me God.

Everyone slits throats and wands are lowered.

HARRINGTON. Having been kept for a considerable time in a
state of darkness, what in your present situation is the pre-
dominant wish of your heart?

BAGLEY. Light.

HARRINGTON. Brother Rochester, let that blessing be restored
to the candidate.

> HARRINGTON *waves his gavel left, right, then down on the
> pedestal. All give a single clap.* ROCHESTER *removes the
> blindfold, directing* BAGLEY's *eyes onto the Bible. He removes
> the noose.*

Brother Alfred Bagley, by your meek and candid behaviour
here this evening, you have escaped two great dangers, those
of stabbing and strangling, for on your entrance into this lodge
this poniard was presented to your naked left breast, so that
had you rashly attempted to rush forward you would have been
accessory to your own death by stabbing. There was likewise
this cable tow with a running noose about your neck which
would have rendered any attempt at retreat equally fatal. But
the danger which will await you until your latest hour is of
having your throat cut across should you improperly disclose
the secrets of Masonry.

You will now take a short pace towards me with your left foot,
bringing the right heel into its hollow. It is in this position that
the secrets of the degree are communicated. They consist of a
sign, a token, and a word.

Place your hand in this position with the thumb extended in
the form of a square to the left of the windpipe. The sign is
given by drawing the hand smartly across the throat and
dropping it to the side.

He demonstrates. BAGLEY *copies him.*

The grip or token is given by a distinct pressure of the thumb on the first joint of the hand. This when regularly given and received serves to distinguish a brother by night as well as by day. (*He demonstrates.*) This grip or token demands a word. A word highly prized among masons as a guard to their privileges. Too much caution therefore cannot be observed in communicating it. It should never be given at length, but always by letters or syllables. To enable you to do which I must first tell you what that word is. It is BOAZ.

BAGLEY. Boaz.

HARRINGTON. B.O.A.Z.

BAGLEY. B.O.A.Z.

HARRINGTON. This word is derived from the left-hand pillar at the porchway or entrance of King Solomon's Temple. So named after Boaz the Great Grandfather of David. Pass, Boaz.

ROCHESTER *leads* BAGLEY *to* EDMUNDS' *pedestal.* BAGLEY *takes the step and makes the sign.*

EDMUNDS. 'Ave you anything to communicate?

BAGLEY. I have. (*He shakes* EDMUNDS' *hand.*)

EDMUNDS. What is this?

BAGLEY. The grip.

EDMUNDS. What does it demand?

BAGLEY. A word.

EDMUNDS. Give me that word.

BAGLEY. At my initiation I was taught to be cautious. I will letter or half it with you.

EDMUNDS. Which you please, begin.

BAGLEY.   B.

EDMUNDS. O.

BAGLEY.   A.

EDMUNDS. Z.

BAGLEY.   Bo.

EDMUNDS. Az.

BAGLEY.   Boaz.

EDMUNDS. Pass, Boaz.

HARRINGTON. You have been initiated. You are now at liberty to retire, in order to restore yourself to your personal comfort.

CLIVE *leads* BAGLEY *away. They all relax, take off their aprons.*

EDMUNDS. And 'oo the 'ell was that?

HARRINGTON. Brother Edmunds, please . . .

EDMUNDS. Another bloody Tory for t'Lodge, I s'pose.

AVON (*scathing*). We all know you're an MP but no politics, Harry, no politics in the Lodge.

EDMUNDS. I know what you bloody Tories are about. Stuffing local Masonry full o' greengrocer, small trader riff-raff, so that when a certain person drops dead of a certain disease another certain person, slimier than the first, will ascend t' wrapping Master's apron round his upper class twit tin leg. I know what you're up to, Avon. So do up your old school tie. Tight. And 'ang yourself from nearest lampost.

ROCHESTER (*to* AVON). Personal approach, James?

EDMUNDS *turns like a music hall artist.*

EDMUNDS. We are the masters now. Goodbye, playmates.

HARRINGTON. May the Great Architect of the Universe forgive you.

EDMUNDS. You've got to be joking.

He goes out, slamming the door.

ROCHESTER. That was terrible. Terrible of Edmunds to mention your – whatsit – Evelyn.

HARRINGTON. I've come to expect it these last six months. I realize I can't command any respect. The world as I've known it is coming to an end. I've been Master of this Lodge for twenty-five years. Through a Depression and a World War.

And now men whom I thought forthright can no longer even mention the name of my disease to me. (HARRINGTON *looks them straight in the eye and shakes their hands.*) James, I think you will be a fine Master of the Lodge. (*He turns before he goes.*) It now seems impossible to ask even for a little – terminal – politeness.

    He goes out. Long pause.

CLIVE. Cancer.

ROCHESTER. Cancer.

BASSETT. Has he been – to Harley Street – again?

AVON. Please. Duncan. It's a matter of weeks.

    Pause.

BASSETT. You reckon you'll get in, don't you, James?

AVON. I'm the Master's choice.

BASSETT. You're not Harry Edmunds' choice. You're going to have to take him by the scruff of the neck. You can't go on doing your gentleman act, James.

AVON. Due processes, Duncan.

ROCHESTER. Alfred Bagley –

AVON. Yes?

ROCHESTER. Wants me to put him up for the Conservative Club. I imagine that means –

CLIVE. Aha, another vote for you in the Lodge, Dad.

AVON. You could say.

CLIVE. Now I know why we elected him.

ROCHESTER. Certainly no other reason –

CLIVE. The first hitchhiker to become a Mason.

BASSETT. Having to scrape 'em up off the street, now, James?

AVON. I don't need to explain to you . . .

BASSETT. Don't bother . . .

CLIVE. Alfred Bagley . . .

AVON. Alfred Bagley is an extremely fine fellow. With only one possible shortcoming.

CLIVE. No teeth.

AVON. Namely that he is so impossibly senile he may very well
die before the Master does, thus buggering the point of the
whole exercise.

The door opens timidly.

BAGLEY. May I . . .

They all rush. BAGLEY *looks knackered and rather vague.*

BASSETT. Oh, well done.
ROCHESTER. Well done. Went very well.
CLIVE. Congratulations.
BASSETT. You're one of us.
AVON. I hope your association with us will be long and happy.

They wait for BAGLEY's *reaction expectantly.*

BAGLEY. What I'm really interested in. I'm really interested in
acquiring property.

Pause.

AVON. Never, old man, we never discuss business in the Lodge.

Pause.

BASSETT. In the bar, Alfred, in the bar.

Blackout.

SCENE FOUR

*Photographs. Sporting occasions. Beaming action shots. Golfing
swings and cheerful crowds. Winners hugging trophies. Music: Bing
Crosby sings 'It went right down the middle'.
Lights up.*

A golf flag pushes up through the stage. A ball rolls to within one foot of the hole. EDMUNDS *strides on very pleased. He stands and calls offstage, his* CADDY *behind him.*

EDMUNDS. Beautiful. Now let's see what the Kremlin can do.

Another ball passes across the stage very fast and goes out. BROWNE *walks in angry, heading towards his ball off.*

BROWNE. Oh shit. Shit. I'm trying hard to fake it, Harry. I'm trying hard to fake pleasure in this meaningless bourgeois game.

EDMUNDS. 'Course you can fake it, Tom Browne. After all that practising, chipping ball down yard into outside lav. Funny be'aviour for a Party Member.

BROWNE. You can laugh all you like, Harry Edmunds. I'm an independent communist now. Nothing to do with the Kremlin. I'm working on my own.

EDMUNDS. Party o' one, Tom? Might be the start of something big.

BROWNE. Look, Harry, you know I want to get into public life. Set myself to work. I can't live my life behind the counter at the Post Office. I want everything I do in my life to have a purpose. I used to think I would spend the whole of my life in draughty halls, pamphleteering, be a crank with a megaphone at the factory gate, be locked in smoke-filled attic rooms, endlessly discussing, dotting the I's – that's what happened to my father – romantic – died cursing his friends for minor misinterpretations of the exact meaning of revolution – that mustn't happen to us, Harry. If that happens to us, God help England. And working people.

EDMUNDS. You want to get on Town Council?

BROWNE. Very much.

EDMUNDS. Then you must learn to thrash about whacking little balls into little 'oles. (*He gestures offstage.* BROWNE *trudges off.*) So you want to be youngest Councillor in Midlands? Mayor of Stanton pushed around in a pram? It may 'appen, Tom.

BROWNE (*off*). I'm sure you could swing it for me. Harry.

The ball comes on again. EDMUNDS *stops it with his foot near the hole.* BROWNE *appears again.*

EDMUNDS. You're going to 'ave to join Lodge, Tom. Won't actually get you on Council. But it won't keep you off. And once you are on, well, Councillors who don't don the apron sometimes find Council slightly 'eavy going.

BROWNE. I didn't know the Masons were that strong.

EDMUNDS. It's not that they're strong. It's just . . . You 'ave to join, that's all.

BROWNE. I'd very much like to be Chairman of Town And Country Planning Committee. I would be very good as Chairman of Town And Country Planning Committee.

EDMUNDS. Naked kind of bugger, aren't you.

BROWNE. As long as it's not hurting you, Harry. Get in there. Burrow like a mole.

EDMUNDS. We've never 'ad a Stalinist chairing Town And Country Planning Committee. But there you are . . .

BROWNE. Does that mean I'm on?

EDMUNDS. The English Social Structure, is a complex and beautiful thing. Interlocking escalators. (EDMUNDS *picks up* BROWNE's *ball.*) Come on, Vladimir Illyich. You'll give me that. On to the twelfth. Tories on next fairway. We've got an appointment.

BROWNE. Where?

EDMUNDS. Fixed a meeting. After many months I 'ave agreed to meet the crazy gang. In an open place. 'Ello! Looks like they're in bunker. Ha Ha.

They go off. The flag disappears. Enter a bunker. AVON, CLIVE *and* ROCHESTER *on its rim looking down on* BASSETT *in the sand.*

AVON. For Godsake, Duncan.

CLIVE. Pathetic.

BASSETT. All I can say is . . . I'm very sorry.

ROCHESTER. Don't tweak that left wrist.

BASSETT. How do you mean?

ROCHESTER. I mean when you . . . tweak.

CLIVE. Look everyone, Edmunds coming through on the fairway.

BASSETT. Where?

ROCHESTER. Concentrate, Duncan. Just concentrate, keep your eye on the ball. And don't tweak.

AVON. Who's that with Edmunds?

CLIVE. It's that unctuous little shit Browne. Shit Browne, ha ha.

BASSETT. Please could you all shut up while I do this?

AVON. Browne?

ROCHESTER. I bet Harry puts him up for the Lodge. Another vote for him.

CLIVE. Blackball him. Little sniveller.

AVON. We can't blackball another one. We've blackballed twelve of Harry's suggestions already. These farcical non-elections are doing us a great deal of harm. The whole tone is lowered.

BASSETT. Please. Sympathize.

BASSETT *strikes the ball and muffs it.*

CLIVE. Pick the sodding thing up and let's get on to the green.

(*They are about to move off.*)

AVON. Linger, gentlemen, linger. Edmunds is upon us.

CLIVE *tosses the ball into the bunker.*

CLIVE. Back into the bunker, Bassett.

BASSETT. But I just got out.

CLIVE. In.

BASSETT. All right. I will 'umiliate myself.

CLIVE. In. Bash it about a bit. Here they come. The red horde.

Everyone pretends to be waiting for BASSETT.

EDMUNDS (*calling from off*). May we come through?

They nod exaggeratedly and smile.

CLIVE (*quietly*). Come through, you fat prick.

Enter EDMUNDS *and* BROWNE.

EDMUNDS. Gentlemen.
AVON. How are you, Harry?
EDMUNDS. Par on the eleventh.
AVON. Congratulations.
EDMUNDS. Clive. Bill. Duncan.
CLIVE. Harry.
BASSETT. Harry.
ROCHESTER. Harry.
BROWNE. Good morning.
EDMUNDS. You all know Browne. And 'ave trembled. At 'is rhetoric.

They all smile except CLIVE.

About to tweak your left wrist, Duncan.
BASSETT. Really? Is that what I'm doing?
EDMUNDS. I've asked Tom if 'e would fancy being in't Lodge.

Pause.

CLIVE. A poor candidate in a state of darkness humbly soliciting . . .
AVON. Do shut up. You didn't hear that, Browne.
BROWNE. No. No.
AVON. I thought I'd have a word with you, Harry. And with some more of the more responsible Worshipful Brothers . . . about the present hiatus in the Lodge.
EDMUNDS. In-deed.
AVON. To be bald, Harry. The Lodge must have a new Master. Business life abhors a vacuum.
EDMUNDS. I follow you.
AVON. These interregnums disturb the . . . (*He searches for a word.*)

ROCHESTER. Charitable work.

AVON. Good work we all do.

EDMUNDS. With you one 'undred per cent.

AVON. So, old man . . .

EDMUNDS. You or me, eh?

AVON. Baldly. Yes.

EDMUNDS. Baldly I'd say . . . me.

All laugh except BROWNE.

AVON. I can't allow a complete Socialist takeover of the town.
You don't even want the Lodge, Harry. You just want to spoil
it for . . . people like us.

EDMUNDS. Are you questioning my sincerity?

AVON ⎱ No.
CLIVE ⎰ Yes.

AVON. No, Clive. You must never question . . . where will we
all be? You know me, Harry . . .

EDMUNDS. I know you, James. (*Pause.*) You're not going to get
Lodge.

Pause.

AVON. I'm going to make a gesture here. Bagley.

EDMUNDS. You what?

AVON. We must both back down. And give it to Bagley.

EDMUNDS. Bagley. Bagley. What's Bagley?

CLIVE. Utter nonentity. Worse than wallpaper.

ROCHESTER. Not one of us.

BASSETT. Man's a complete idiot. Dribbles!

ROCHESTER. We've got to keep it for people like us . . . Other-
wise what's the point?

AVON. We could do far worse than Bagley.

EDMUNDS. Frankly I'd be disappointed. But I like the idea of it
not being you.

AVON. Bagley is by no means a bad person. For either of us. He has – and this will please you, Harry – no visible public school education. But on our side we are willing to pass lightly over this – one's mind has been broadened by the war – for he does now enjoy a sound financial basis in the town. Nothing spectacular. Nothing that will make him too pushy. Nothing to embarrass either of us. A decent, quiet stopgap who I think we will find will plug most of the holes.

ROCHESTER. Superb.

CLIVE. You have skated round his one major asset –

AVON. Quiet, Clive. (*Then to* EDMUNDS.) As Clive says there is one other thing about Mr Bagley. He is very old.

CLIVE. Senile.

EDMUNDS. With you. Bound to die.

Pause.

AVON. What do you say, Harry?

EDMUNDS. Mmmmmm . . . What I say is: Mmmmmm . . . (*Pause. Then decisively.*) I want Tom Browne in Lodge. I want him unopposed in next Council by-election. I want an embargo on free debate about 'is political past. And everyone to be nice to 'im.

　　　AVON *smiles at once.*

AVON. Hallo, Tom.

EDMUNDS. Done.

AVON. Done.

EDMUNDS. Lovely.

　　　AVON *shakes hands with* BROWNE. *Then* ROCHESTER *does, and* CLIVE.

AVON. Harry. Let's have a real discussion now . . . a more serious talk . . .

EDMUNDS. Right.

AVON. Caddy, take my clubs. We'll walk.

CADDY. Sir.

AVON *and* EDMUNDS *begin to walk.*

AVON. Now Harry, local affairs in general. And more specifically the business community. Your attitude to labour disputes. And how you can help us in areas where the long . . . arm of . . . government . . . touches . . .

    EDMUNDS *puts his arm round* AVON *and they walk off talking.*

ROCHESTER. Just like the old days.

CLIVE. A place in the sun.

BASSETT. Can I get out of the bunker now?

ROCHESTER (*warmly*). Of course, Duncan, I'm sorry.

    BASSETT *brushes his trousers.*

BASSETT. Bloody desert warfare.

    He goes out.

BROWNE. Er. Well. Good morning.

ROCHESTER. Invite him to lunch.

CLIVE. You invite him to lunch.

ROCHESTER. Not me.

CLIVE. You.

ROCHESTER (*going over to* BROWNE.) Clive and I wondered if you'd like a spot of lunch with us. (ROCHESTER *turns back to* CLIVE *beaming.* CLIVE *makes a face.*)

BROWNE. Thank you. That would be most . . . exciting.

    Pause. They look at him. He reaches in his pocket.

  Cigar?

CLIVE. Thank you. I'll have mine . . . after lunch.

ROCHESTER. Oh God. Shouldn't somebody tell Bagley?

CLIVE. What?

ROCHESTER. His good fortune.

CLIVE. Master of the Lodge. We have a new Master.

    Huge decadent fanfare.
    Blackout.

SCENE FIVE

The stage bursts into colour. The Vatican. A huge altar and golden angels.
As the lights come up a mad CARDINAL *is screaming at the audience at the front of the stage.*

CARDINAL. Veni cum jubilate laudem. Habemus pontificem! Habemus pontificem! A great new Holy Father.

A second CARDINAL *runs screaming on to the stage.*

SECOND CARDINAL. Ooo izzy? Ooo izzy?
CARDINAL. 'E is Borja. We have a new Pope. Alonso de Borja.
SECOND CARDINAL. Borja Borja.

> *Huge whispers all over the theatre, 'BORJA, BORJA, BORJA,' which rise and then explode into music. A huge organ burst.*
> *Narrow light on* ALFRED BAGLEY *dressed as* CALLISTUS III, *sitting on an enormous throne in a cloud of incense, his hand resting on a small white* HERMAPHRODITE.

BAGLEY. You have turned in your hour of need to an old man. One of the least of you God has made the greatest among you. Sick as we are of the debased, debasing warring factions within the Vatican, yet are we now ready to smile upon the defeated families, ready to receive them into the greater purpose of the greater state, into the divine task of maintaining the sanctity of the Citadel. This is God's work. This I must do. (*He stretches out his hand.*) I want to put my hand on your heads.

At once station announcer in Midland accent.

ANNOUNCER. The train now standing at Platform 5 is the 3.14 stopping train for Crewe.

Blackout.

ANNOUNCER. Calling at Milton Bassett Halt, Ashbourne, Bradnop, Leek, Biddulph, Church Lawton, Winterley, and Crewe. The 3.14 stopping train for Crewe.

SCENE SIX

At once Stanton railway station. Noises of trains and whistles. Steam.
A family wander on. LUCY BAGLEY, 14, angelic, golden curls, like Shirley Temple. SIDNEY BAGLEY, 15, dressed in Eton school uniform, thin and pimply. MARTIN BAGLEY, 12, in short trousers, rather fat, a backward boy pulling a fluffy dog on wheels on the end of a long string. Then RODERICK BAGLEY, 37, an unsmiling man with an air of authority that doesn't quite work.

RODERICK. Porter. My bags, please.

A PORTER comes across to pick up the suitcases.

SIDNEY. Where's your Spitfire, Martin?
MARTIN. Here. It's got a little pilot in the cockpit.
RODERICK. A taxi, please. Porter.

He tips him. LUCY sidles up to the PORTER and pouts.

LUCY. Hello, porter.

She lifts her skirt slightly. MARTIN gets out a model Spitfire.

RODERICK. Lucy! You must not do that to every strange man you meet.

SIDNEY. Battle of Britain. Shall we play Battle of Britain?

MARTIN. Yes, please.

SIDNEY. What you do is – put the Spitfire down on the ground –

> MARTIN *puts it down, circling.*

MARTIN. Vroom – vroom –

SIDNEY. Right – now – look – you're in the Spitfire – all right Martin?

MARTIN. Prrr Prrr.

SIDNEY. And I'm the German Luftwaffe. (*He jumps on the model and crushes it with his boot.*)

LUCY. Look. There's a Ticket Inspector.

MARTIN (*dissolves into a sob*). Aaaah.

RODERICK. What have you been doing, Sidney?

SIDNEY. Martin's Spitfire got shot down. (SIDNEY *kicks it off stage.*) In the English Channel.

LUCY (*heading off stage*). Hullo, Ticket Inspector.

RODERICK. Lucy.

> Enter VANESSA BAGLEY, 36, *thin and in a floral summer frock. With flower brooches.*

VANESSA. Don't take it to heart, Martin. What is it?

MARTIN (*sobs*). My plane.

RODERICK. Are we going to the hospital first or are we going straight to the hotel?

VANESSA. Did you do that to Martin's aeroplane?

SIDNEY. It was an impulse.

RODERICK. Vanessa, am I to make this decision or am I not?

VANESSA. Martin, can you blow your nose?

RODERICK. Right. Hospital. And everyone behave. The old man'll be dead before we get there. Where is that taxi?

> ALFRED BAGLEY *appears in a black overcoat. Fitter and louder than he has been before.*

BAGLEY. Hallo, Roderick.

They stare at him. Pause. LUCY *goes up to him.*

LUCY. Hello, old man.

She lifts her skirt up slightly. He at once puts his arm round her and gathers her up in a kiss.

BAGLEY. Hello, Lucy. (*He now has a Midlands accent.*)

LUCY. We travelled First Class.

BAGLEY. Of course you did, love. (*Pause.*) Your Dad's staring at me. Hello, Roderick.

RODERICK. Uncle. We thought you were on your way.

BAGLEY. What?

RODERICK. Dying. I've ordered a taxi . . .

BAGLEY. Oh, I walked out of hospital days ago.

RODERICK. But you sent a telegram. 'Dying. Come. Now. Alfred.'

BAGLEY. I thought I'd use my death to best advantage.

BAGLEY *goes over to* SIDNEY *and* MARTIN.

Hello, Sidney, last time I saw you you were in short trousers. Hello, Martin, you still are in short trousers.

He kisses them on the top of the head. VANESSA *hovers hopelessly.*

VANESSA. So glad the flowers won't be necessary.

He kisses her.

BAGLEY. Welcome to Stanton, Roderick. (*He holds out his hand. They shake,* RODERICK *stiffly.*)

RODERICK. Well, I suppose we take the taxi to the hotel. Not the hospital after all.

BAGLEY. There's a train back in twenty minutes. Unless.

The PORTER *has returned.*

PORTER. Yer taxi, sir.

RODERICK. Unless?

BAGLEY. I married a barren woman, Roderick.

PORTER. Yer taxi, sir.

BAGLEY. No children. You're my nearest. I've been watering you, Roderick. All that money. These last three years.

VANESSA. We've been terribly grateful for your help with Sidney's school fees. And for getting Roderick through night class.

RODERICK. It is not night class. It is an Architectural Diploma I happen to work on in the evening.

LUCY. We all hope Daddy's going to pass.

RODERICK. Shut up, Lucy.

LUCY. Secretly I hope he's going to fail.

BAGLEY (to LUCY). If he fails I think I'll demand my money back. But he won't fail, unless he wants to spend the rest of his life in the Maths department at Ealing grammar. Eating 'imself out with unfulfilled ambition. (He turns.) Will he, Roderick?

SIDNEY *is lying on the ground looking up* LUCY's *skirt.*

RODERICK. Vanessa, tell Sidney I'm going to hit him in a minute.

PORTER. Tickin' on meter.

RODERICK. This is a private conversation. Please stand back.

The PORTER *shrugs.*

BAGLEY. A choice, Roderick. At this heady moment. I have some small property holdings in Stanton, a town of 40,000 souls. Houses and rented accommodation I've accumulated over the last three years. But I don't feel I've brought enough to the life of the town. Yet. I'm a landlord. Pure and simple. But Bagleys should be builders. Over the last three years there's been something of a spiral in rents. Which means I've been able to acquire more land. Now as I've acquired the land I've ploughed the money back into puffing you up to the status of Architect. And now I want to marry my land with your expertise. (Pause.) Chuck up your job in that school. Moonlight flit. Bump yourself up in the world. Make a myth.

VANESSA. Leave Ealing, darling?

RODERICK. Only . . .

BAGLEY. Yes?

RODERICK. On my own terms.

BAGLEY. Of course.

RODERICK. My firm.

BAGLEY. Of course.

RODERICK. My name.

BAGLEY. Of course. Boards on building sites. 'Roderick Bagley Associates.'

RODERICK. Yes. Yes. I like it.

BAGLEY. Office to yourself. See less of the family. With a bit of luck.

RODERICK. Something massive. And straightforward. A great many men. A great deal of . . . yes. Great deal of well directed effort. Honest toil and welcome reward. Everyone having a job to do. And taking a pride.

BAGLEY. Knew you had it in you. (*He gestures.*) God's own Englishman.

SIDNEY *empties lighter fuel over* MARTIN's *fluffy dog, unseen by all.*

RODERICK. I've always admired decisive behaviour. Without having had . . . much opportunity myself.

VANESSA. I hope it's not a dirty town to live in.

BAGLEY (*to the* PORTER). We don't need a taxi. Got a car of our own.

BAGLEY *holds out a folded note between fingers.* PORTER *takes it. Then* BAGLEY *waves hugely at someone offstage.*

VANESSA. Will we be able to bring the greenhouse North? After forcing the dahlias all winter?

RODERICK. How will the locals feel about us?

BAGLEY. Oh the gentry. Dozy. Divine Right Brigade. Divine Right to build . . . and to be builded over . . .

The PHOTOGRAPHER *enters with camera. The family all pose.*

BAGLEY. Local press. Come on. All of you. Family photograph.
The old man gathers his family around him.

> BAGLEY *takes* RODERICK's *hand.* BAGLEY *and* RODERICK
> *turn and smile at the camera.* MARTIN's *dog bursts into flames.*
> SIDNEY *and* LUCY *laugh. The camera flashes.*

MARTIN. My dog's on fire.

Blackout.

SCENE SEVEN

*Photographs. Food queues. Ration Book. A sign reading : 'This mine
now managed by the government on behalf of the people.' Slum houses
1945–1950. Music : Ann Shelton sings 'Lay Down Your Arms'.
Lights up.*

*Derelict room of an old house. Very run down. No furniture. A
pram. Strips of old-fashioned wallpaper. A small grate. Water
visible on the back wall.*
JAMES AVON *is already on, cheerful.*

BAGLEY (*off*). Do you like it?
AVON. It's magnificent.
BAGLEY (*off*). Think it'll do?
AVON. It'll do fine.
BAGLEY (*off*). When we've knocked it down.
AVON. Yes. Nice area.

> BAGLEY *appears at the door. Stands in the frame. Homburg
> now as well as black coat.*

BAGLEY. First properties I bought from you. When I came to

Stanton, four years ago. (*He feels the doorframe.*) Sentimental. Tear in my eye today.

AVON (*smiles*). Alf.

> BAGLEY *takes his homburg off and runs his finger round the leather rim.* SIDNEY *comes in with two orange boxes for them to sit on.*

AVON. We feel so affectionate . . . towards you.

BAGLEY. Least I can do. Selling my first and favourite houses to the Council to build Hospital.

AVON. It's much appreciated.

BAGLEY. Self-interest.

AVON (*smiles*). What do you mean?

BAGLEY. I'll need 'Ospital some time. In the next forty years.

> BAGLEY *and* AVON *laugh together.*

AVON. Alf. No. Genuinely . . . kind.

BAGLEY. Slums anyway.

AVON. Well – I must be getting home for tea.

BAGLEY. Stay a moment. Humour an old man. (BAGLEY *nods at* SIDNEY.)

SIDNEY. So long, gents.

> SIDNEY *goes out.*

AVON. Your great nephew dresses rather . . . loudly.

BAGLEY. He's a Franky boy. You know, Frank Sinatra. The hat. (*Pause.*) It's Sidney's father I'm hoping will build the Hospital.

AVON. Oh, that would be very good. Be very satisfying for your family. Round things off.

BAGLEY. That's what I thought.

AVON. It's a matter of whether Roderick can come up with a suitably attractive plan. Something of the sheer quality of which the town could be proud.

BAGLEY. I understood . . . it was more a matter of expense. Who could put in the lowest tender.

AVON. And do the work.

BAGLEY. Oh, the work must be done. Undeniably.

AVON. The tender is important . . .

BAGLEY. It's the clincher. And Roderick Bagley Architectural Associates are the masters of the lowest tender.

AVON. That is to be seen.

BAGLEY. I have seen it.

AVON. Crystal ball, Alfred?

BAGLEY. If you like.

They smile.

AVON. My son Clive will of course tender for the hospital contract.

BAGLEY. He will. He will. (*Pause.*) But a little too high. (*Pause.*) If there's any justice in the world.

AVON. If there's any justice in the world, my son Clive will build the hospital.

BAGLEY. Take the word of an old man. There is no justice in the world, James. Look at your leg. And his.

Pause. AVON *is amazed.*

AVON. Clive is a far more experienced architect. He was also an officer in the Royal Air Force.

BAGLEY. Roderick may be a bit green, but he's bunged up a fair number of bricks in the last few years. A private estate for me. And work for the Council.

AVON. Three public conveniences in six months. And all within walking distance of each other. There has been talk about that.

BAGLEY. You don't understand anything, James. The subject of the discussion.

AVON. And what is that, Alfred?

BAGLEY. New-fangledness. New approaches, new ways of looking at things. New ways of organizing public contracts. Now take Hospital. We've all got to put our tenders in, and the lowest always gets the job. But here's the new way, James. (*Very quiet.*) We all put our tenders in. But first everyone reveals them to me. I reveal them to Roderick. Who puts in last. And lowest. And wins.

AVON. That's outrageous.

BAGLEY. Then, when he's won, I foresee: problems on site, weather, that sort of thing, costs will rise during the building, we'll have to revise the estimates. Revise the profits. Slightly. Often. Upwards.

AVON. Fiddle? Shennanigans on a public contract? I can only excuse your remarks on the grounds of senility. (*Pause.*) Good God. Clive would never take part. It's inconceivable he would show you his tender, corruptly. Clive enjoys an enviable reputation in this town for absolute integrity.

BAGLEY. Sidney.

SIDNEY *comes in at once.*

SIDNEY. Nuncle.

BAGLEY. Sidney has been listening at the door so he knows what point discussion's reached. Sidney.

SIDNEY *has a large yellow envelope. He takes out an X-ray.*

An X-ray of your son's foot.

SIDNEY *shows it to* AVON, *agape.*

Your son has put it about that he left active service in the RAF in the autumn of '43. Because of a wound. Gallantly received over Germany. Nightfighter strafed the Lancaster in which he was Navigator. He is very modest. Asked about his terrible experience, he makes a wry jest about foxtrotting. (*Pause.* BAGLEY *points.*) Wounds compatible with a Boy Scout knife. (*Change.*) Stabbed it, didn't he, Jim? To get off. Sonnyboy wasn't over Germany. He was on compassionate leave. Out of his mind. With fear.

Pause.

Personally I don't blame the lad. You wouldn't have got me up there . . . Saw a row of bomber boys in a music hall once. Interspersed with beautiful girls. Girls keeping their eyes on the stage. For each bomber boy had his face blown away. (*He runs his hand over his face.*) Sticks with you. Eh James? I don't blame him. But not everyone's as compassionate as me. I'm afraid. He's a coward, if everyone knows. And your own leg will be called into question. (*Pause.*) Ribaldry and contempt. (*Pause.*) How you doing? (*Pause.*) Thank you, Sidney.

SIDNEY. Dig.

BAGLEY. And go away.

> SIDNEY *goes out, taking the folder.*

Never believe he's at Eton, would you? (BAGLEY *gets an envelope out of his pocket.*) Just scribble Clive's likely tender, will you?

AVON. You sleazy old man. You. Vicious. Old cad. You will never work your will on this town, because you will never be allowed real power. You will never get on the Council.

BAGLEY. I don't want to run the brothel, son. I just want the girls.

AVON. To be blackmailed . . .

BAGLEY. Quiet, lad.

AVON. To be had. All right. My God. If that weren't enough . . . but to be blackmailed in a fake Midland accent . . .

BAGLEY. Town's grown on me. I'm a romantic. (*Pause.*) Scribble.

> AVON *does so.* BAGLEY *snatches it smartly.*

Good day's work. Grand new hospital.

AVON. And we were going to name it Bagley Hospital.

BAGLEY. We'll call it Avon Hospital then. Fair's fair. (*Pause.*) Time you went home for your tea.

AVON. Yes. (AVON *gets up and starts to go out.*)

BAGLEY. And send Sidney in, will you?

> AVON *opens the door and* SIDNEY *is there. He brushes by.* SIDNEY *comes in, leaves door open.*

BAGLEY. My mother used to describe heaven to me when I was a child. In this way. Heaven is a place where we will be 'at play in the fields of the Lord'. (*Pause.*) Little houses. Little bricks. (*Pause.*) New method worked, Sidney. You'd better tell your Dad to build up his firm overnight. Like a mushroom. Tell him to get some real architects to help him. Quantity Surveyors, get some of those. All the paraphernalia. Sub-tender. Sub-contract. Rod'll enjoy that. Being a late bloom. (*He smiles.*) I'm going to cram a silver spoon down your throat.

SIDNEY (*grandly*). I admire this man.

> *Blackout.*

SCENE EIGHT

Photographs. The Coronation 1953. Coach, Queen, Queen Mother, Duke of Edinburgh. Everest climbed. The Abbey. The Royal group. Music: Crown Imperial.

Lights up on a huge wedding table in a tent. It is laid elaborately with flowers. At the back a table laden with food and drink. LUCY *runs on in a white wedding dress, being chased by* ROCHESTER, CLIVE, EDMUNDS, *and* BASSETT *all in morning dress.* BASSETT *is carrying a rose bush with earth on its roots.* LUCY *jumps on to a table.*

LUCY. My day. My day. I'm wet. Wet all down me.

CLIVE. We can smell it from here.

BASSETT (*very drunk*). There's steam coming off it. And a smell of bananas.

LUCY. Champers all down me.

ROCHESTER. I'll say this for her . . . she's a slip of a girl.

LUCY. Who wants a lick? (LUCY *curtseys.*) Gentlemen.

> RODERICK *comes in.*

RODERICK. Gentlemen. Please, everyone. We are in a tent. I don't want to say anything, but a flowerbed has already been denuded. And trampled on. If there were some simple rules – like – no cigarettes stubbed on the lawn. Thank you. Relavatories, there is a canvas pissoir under the elms. I mention no names. I am very anxious you should all enjoy yourselves. But please . . . that's all . . . please.

VANESSA. Don't get too over-excited, darling.

ROCHESTER. She's a sliver of a girl . . . wish my daughter was like that.

VANESSA. You know you get flushed. And you've still got two hundred guests to kiss.

BASSETT. We've kissed her already and now we're going to lick her, Mrs Bagley.

VANESSA (*with dignity*). Thank you, Mr Bassett. (*She turns away.*) Oh dear.

LUCY. It's my bloody day.

AVON *has entered. Now* RODERICK *comes in again.*

RODERICK. Where is the groom? Lucy, have you seen your husband?

LUCY. Of one hour's standing.

EDMUNDS. You should be so lucky.

RODERICK. Vanessa.

LUCY. I saw him last night. Wrapped round my middle.

EDMUNDS. As the saying goes.

AVON (*to* CLIVE). There you have it. Animal behaviour.

CLIVE. Yes, Dad. Go and get drunk.

AVON *wanders away.*

RODERICK. Where is he?

BASSETT. What's the matter?

EDMUNDS. The Bagleys 'ave mislaid the groom.

BASSETT. Rabbit popped out of bag?

LUCY. How should I know?

ROCHESTER. They won't let him go now.

EDMUNDS. When they got one in the gin-trap they got 'im. Cut to the bone.

VANESSA. I think I saw Dennis, dear, going into the chemical toilet.

CLIVE. Strapping a new cock on.

BASSETT. Well done, Mrs Bagley. Said 'toilet' to us all.

MARTIN has come on.

RODERICK. Martin. Off you go.

MARTIN hesitates.

Go and find Dennis. In the lavatory. And bring him here.

MARTIN. Yes, Dad.

Pause. Everyone looks at MARTIN.

MARTIN. Now?

RODERICK. Yes. Off you go.

MARTIN goes slowly off.

CLIVE. You're looking . . .

LUCY. Yes, Clive?

CLIVE. You're looking rather wonderful. In your way.

LUCY. It's an inner light, Clive.

CLIVE. I see.

LUCY. Shining where you'll never go.

RODERICK. Let's get this organized. There are table napkins –

ROCHESTER
BASSETT   } (*in chorus, singing*). I'm dreaming of a tight mistress . . .
EDMUNDS

CLIVE. Tonight Dennis Macpherson, Dougal to his friends, will tread where no man has ever trod before. In boots.

MEN (*singing*). Just like the ones I used to know . . .

RODERICK. Now everyone: there are table napkins.

A MAJORDOMO has entered.

MAJORDOMO. Ladies and gentlemen, pray silence for the Right
  Worshipful Mayor of Stanton, Alderman Mr Thomas Browne.

Enter TOM BROWNE, *in mayoral robes and chain.*

BROWNE. No, please, everyone, don't stop for me. Just carry on.
  Be happy. Happy day. (*Going over to* LUCY.) My gift's a fridge.
  Gold fridge. Not solid gold. I'm only Mayor. Painted gold.
  But I put six chickens inside.
LUCY. Thank you, Tom. You've got to be kissed now.
BROWNE. Hope the groom's not watching.
EDMUNDS. 'E's not.

Enter SIDNEY.

SIDNEY. Hey lads, I've plugged up a goggle-box in the house.
CLIVE. Great.
SIDNEY. They're just going to crown Queenie.
EDMUNDS. 'Ey quick. Let's get a butcher's. Thought I was
  going to miss it.

A dirty rush for the door.

BASSETT. What's going on?
CLIVE. Coronation, come on.
RODERICK. Hold on, everyone.
CLIVE. Won't be long.
RODERICK. Please. Manners. Please.

EDMUNDS *turns back.*

EDMUNDS. Just . . . talk among yourselves.

He goes off.

RODERICK. This is Uncle Alfred's fault. It was his idea to have
  his darling Lucy marry today. My dear. Just for a headline.
  Bagley Coronation Wedding Today. Where is he anyway?
VANESSA. Watching the television.
RODERICK. Rude old man.

RODERICK *touches* LUCY.

My dear.

LUCY *hits him.*

LUCY. You wouldn't stand up to him, would you? You wouldn't dare not play his games?

RODERICK. Why don't you leave me alone? Why can't everyone leave me alone?

RODERICK *storms out into the TV room.*

VANESSA. It does seem a shame to miss it, dear.

LUCY. Well, off you go.

VANESSA. Be happy.

VANESSA *goes out.* LUCY *alone. From offstage we hear Dimbleby and the Archbishop at the Abbey. The Queen is crowned. Pause.*

LUCY. And when I was married . . .

She picks up an eclair and slams it into her mouth. Cream dribbles. MARTIN *enters very quietly.*

MARTIN. Dennis is being sick in the lavatory.

LUCY (*gently*). Thank you, Martin.

MARTIN. Is it over?

LUCY. What are you looking at me like that for?

MARTIN. I think you're making a beautiful . . . exhibition of yourself.

LUCY. Thank you, brother.

MARTIN. I think I'm being . . . looked at. Like the rest of the family. Do you think I should do . . . something unusual?

LUCY. Like what?

MARTIN. Like . . . dance with you?

LUCY. A naked polka?

MARTIN. Something like that . . .

LUCY. I know how you feel. (*Pause.*) When are you getting married, Martin?

MARTIN. I've not . . . met anyone I love, yet. (*Pause.*) Dennis said, in the little lavatory tent, he didn't care if the ground swallowed him up, just so long as he never came near you again. Do you love him?

LUCY. His father's in biscuits. Scottish biscuits. Millions and millions of Scottish biscuits. There's always a plate of short-bread by the bed. And crumbs in my knickers.

MARTIN. You come . . . Like . . . Very odd.

LUCY. But beautiful. I'll get you your Mummy. (*She sweeps away and calls.*) Mum! Come out of that house. Martin's having one of his things! (*She turns back to* MARTIN). So get back in here!

ALFRED BAGLEY *comes on, good humoured.*

BAGLEY. Come on, everyone. Back to the boring old wedding.

Everyone pours back, all twelve of them including the MAJOR-DOMO *who stands at the back. Everyone is very excited.*

Surprised at you, Lucy, not wanting to see your new Queen.

MARTIN. I'm not . . . having one of my things, at all.

VANESSA. The Queen Mother bore up wonderfully in the wet. She's like . . . a proud galleon in stormy seas.

BASSETT. That crown looked heavy. God it was heavy.

CLIVE. As Dimbleby ceaselessly pointed out.

EDMUNDS. She must 'ave been in pain. (*He gestures to the back of his neck.*) Right 'ere.

BAGLEY. That moment. A great moment. The peak of the occasion. When that very old Archbishop, that venerable man, grasped that great weight . . . (*He demonstrates.*) Held it in the air, as the Abbey seemed to breathe, then . . . (*Pause.*) Plonked it on her head.

EDMUNDS. She could 'ave cricked 'er neck. (*He gestures to the back of his neck.*) Right 'ere.

VANESSA. Oh yes, the day was fraught with peril for her, wasn't it, Mr Edmunds?

EDMUNDS. I'm sorry, love, I'm pissed out of my mind.

RODERICK. Everyone gather round now.

LUCY. From what you all say she sounds very beautiful on the little grey tube.

VANESSA. Alka-Seltzer?

BAGLEY. Little madam.

LUCY *pouts.* BAGLEY *hits her bottom.*

RODERICK. You've all got marked places.

VANESSA. Golden day.

BAGLEY (*to* LUCY). Shall I pick you up?

LUCY *jumps into* BAGLEY'*s arms.*

LUCY. Whirl me, Uncle.

RODERICK. You will find your names on your napkin rings. No, the napkin rings are to the right of your places, Duncan.

BASSETT. Stuff yourself.

BAGLEY *is whirling* LUCY *around as everyone goes to their places.*

MAJORDOMO. May we begin?

RODERICK. Ask my Uncle.

The MAJORDOMO *tries to speak to the whirling* BAGLEY.

BASSETT. Doesn't the groom have any family?

ROCHESTER. Couldn't make it, old man.

MAJORDOMO. Mr Bagley, may we begin?

CLIVE. There *was* a groom, I think.

BASSETT. Couldn't see from my seat. Bagley put me behind a pillar.

ROCHESTER. Chap in a kilt.

MAJORDOMO. Mr Bagley, surely we . . .

BAGLEY. Get him to read out menu.

    BAGLEY *sits down and bangs the table.*

What are we 'aving?

    RODERICK *picks up the menu.*

RODERICK. Read that out? Loud and clear.

MAJORDOMO. Sir.

BAGLEY. Let them cost it up.

MAJORDOMO. Soupe de L'Oignon Gratinée aux Crevettes au Grand Marnier.

EDMUNDS. What?

BASSETT. Soup, you dumb bugger.

EDMUNDS. Nice.

MAJORDOMO. Poulet farci aux rognons de porc et truffes noires de Perigord avec les Haricots du Tour d'Argent, et les Pommes de Terre Pont Royal.

BAGLEY (*quietly*). The weight.

MAJORDOMO. Marrons glacés au crème chantilly au fond de pêche et des noisettes de la Rive Gauche.

BAGLEY. The weight. On the young woman's head. The weight on the young woman's shoulders. The weight on the young woman's breasts.

    A long embarrassed pause.

VANESSA. I do wish Dennis were here.

RODERICK. Martin did you go and . . .

    BAGLEY *suddenly is up on his feet.*

BAGLEY. I'm going to make my speech now.

VANESSA. After the meal, Uncle.

BAGLEY. My speech begins . . . (*Pause.* BAGLEY *takes out notes and reads.*)

BAGLEY. On-this-happy-day. How-happy-we-all-are. Her-mother-always-says-Lucy's-got-my-nose. How-happy-am-I-that-that's-so.

VANESSA *titters, and looks to the company.* ROCHESTER *titters, no one else.*

Jokes-apart, I-hope-to-see-before-too-long-who-knows-how-many - little - great-great - nephews - and - great-great - nieces - running-about-all-with-my-nose.

ROCHESTER *at once titters and* VANESSA *looks at him, worried.*

But-I-did-say-jokes-apart. All-my-life . . . (BAGLEY *turns over his notes and gets the pages wrong.*) I-have-taken-this-town-by-the-throat. (*Dead silence.*) Oh. (*He reorganizes his notes laboriously, then looks up with a bright eye.*) Shuffled pack wrong. Came up with joker.

All laugh.

I-was-born-

All shut up.

In 1872. James my brother came three years later. In 1886 I left this town to go to London. I worked as a clerk in a warehouse. Of a retail hosier. It was rough for a young man. The first day one of the other clerks said to me, 'Bagley, go down to the General Office and ask the Chief Clerk if you can collect the long weight.' I went down to the General Office and said, 'I have been sent for the long weight.' 'Very well,' said the Chief Clerk. I stood there for an hour or more not daring to utter a sound. After the hour had gone by the Chief Clerk had still said nothing. So I piped up. 'Can I have the long weight?' And the Chief Clerk said, 'You've had it.'

ROCHESTER *tries to laugh but* BAGLEY *ploughs on.*

Married my departed . . . dear departed wife Angela on the last day of April 1908. Then it was spring blossoms for her posy. She had a milliner's shop which I sold to acquire, with the help of my saved and scrimped little pile, a drapery business.

Bed clothes. All to do with linen. Angela hankered after hats. But I knew that with lady's trade you could be left by fashion high and dry on the beach. Bones picked clean. Angela hankered after the fancy work with her hands, which were very fine-fingered. But we are born to bear reproaches. Nevertheless she contented herself to every Easter making a hat, till in 1943, the year she died, my dear cherished wife had thirty-three such hats. I burnt the hats on a bombsite the day after she died. For I tell the young ones here today, never break your heart.

Though barren ourselves, we were joyed to see my brother James married, Roddy's father. And Roddy came soon after. There's very little that matters in the world. Family's a warm overcoat. And in 1914 Great War broke out.

BAGLEY *turns a page. Polite bored coughs.*

When I got back from War I was a changed man. You see when War came in 1914 none of us knew what the world was like. We did not know the full extent to which mankind can go. Many a comrade fell. There is a foreign field which is forever. I went to France in all ignorance thinking of picking up a bit of French linen. I came back with my whole philosophical outlook. But I continued to be a draper and just in time before the depression opened a second shop and moved to Pinner.

BASSETT *gives a loud sigh.*

About this time my nephew Roderick now so prosperous and here before you got his first job in Ealing schoolmastering. And quickly in succession came his wife Vanessa, the marriage was 1931, and 1932 came Sidney, and 1933 came Lucy and 1935 came little Martin. Then Hitler came along. One day we were going down into the air-raid shelter. Angela slipped and hit her head on the stone step.

BAGLEY *turns over a page. But he does not read from it. Instead he drifts and drops the paper.*

What I'd like to give you, today, is my . . . impressions and deductions I have made . . . For example, in the Great World War, I saw a man eating . . . you know, human flesh . . .

Pause. VANESSA *pales.*

Long pork, we called it . . . What were tasty were human brain . . . if rats didn't get there before we English Tommies. (ROCHESTER *rushes out.*) Funny, having to go to war t' see inside o' human brain for first time. And me a man in middle life . . . If I'd had a son, I'd have said this to him 'bout Great War . . . I don't know how we did not all go mad . . . I didn't . . . I came home normal . . . With a bit o' French satin for my featherbrained wife, to sew into an outdated hat, which she did . . . duly . . . normal . . . hard as nails . . . and braced . . . and me a healthy mature man, normal as the garden path . . . in our house in Pinner . . . Walking down the garden path . . . a man who's seen another gnawing a human bone just like a knuckle of ham . . . Long walk, straight down the garden path . . . like my hitchhike eight years ago to this town . . . walked through half o' England and in my seventy-seventh year . . . long long walk . . . long long wait . . .

BAGLEY *laughs and slaps his thigh. Everyone surprised.*

In my long life nothing's touched me. No one's touched me! E-state agents, architects, newly-weds, cannibals, none of you. (*Chirpily, the accent returning.*) Clever young reporter from the local rag t'other day . . . asked me if I were a nihilist. I asked him what he meant, you know, playing daft. Man who believes in nothing, the youngster said. And do you know what, you good people here . . . I felt like giving him a quid for hitting jackpot . . . But joking apart, I gave him a quid and sent him away. (*Silence. He is staring down.*) But . . . but . . . but . . . but . . . (*He wags his finger.*) Cr. Cr. Cr. Cr . . . I've got a beady eye. Cr . . . Cr . . . Cr . . . Cr . . . goes the crow on't gate . . . Dirty old crow. Believing nothing . . . thinking nothing, but with a beady eye for . . . (*He suddenly shoots his hand out and points at* AVON.) T'WORM.

RODERICK. Uncle, I think we would all be very pleased if you stuck more closely to the text of your speech.

BAGLEY *eyes everyone viciously and smacks his lips.*

BAGLEY. Crooooooow.

RODERICK *leans over quickly and snatches the last page of the speech up from the table and shoves it in the hands of the* MAJORDOMO.

RODERICK. You. Read that out.

BAGLEY. To bitter end o' garden path.

RODERICK (*to* VANESSA). Drunk, you know.

BAGLEY (*at* VANESSA). Crow?

MAJORDOMO. And-some-do-say-I-have-taken-this-town-by-the -throat - but - all - I - have - done - is - for - my - family - and - who - can - blame - an - old - fool - for - putting - on - a - warm - snug-overcoat-against-t'-cold.

God - bless - you - Lucy - and - to - joke - apart - since - mar- riage - is - like - a - boat - God - bless - thee - Lucy - 'lass' - and - all-who-sail-in-thee.

RODERICK *starts applauding and stands. No response. He sits down.*

VANESSA *stands bravely.*

VANESSA. I think . . .

BASSETT *stands and claps her.* ROCHESTER *returns.*

VANESSA. I think we all remember that moment in the nursery when we've been having a lot of fun and somebody goes a little too far and says something very silly, which they don't really mean and which tomorrow they're going to wish they hadn't said. So let's pass on from the speeches and the telegrams to . . . (*She loses her thread.*) Pass onto . . . onto . . .

CLIVE. *Really* having a bash at each other.

*All the non-*BAGLEYS *laugh.*

BASSETT (*to* AVON). Hallo, worm.

BAGLEY *and* LUCY *are in a world of their own.*

BAGLEY. Little Lucy.
LUCY. What's the matter?
BAGLEY. Little Lucy.

AVON *suddenly stands up.*

AVON. What do you mean – worm? Worm? Worm? Why should
I sit here slopping at your trough? Among men I've known for
fifteen, for fifty years. You have slandered all of us. Let me
reply: the bride is a prostitute.
BASSETT (*low*). Heads down. Over the wire.
AVON. No less. No more. And a good deal more. You are trying
to drag us all down to your level. Apparently to the level of
cannibals. Well, I have to live with myself. I have to go home
and live with my wife. And when she asks how was the wedding?
I shall be morally forced to reply: the pus. The pus flowed.
(*Pause. He walks to the tent exit. Dignity.*) But I will be able to
comfort myself with the fact I left. I left before things really
ripped apart.

The entrance is opened. SIDNEY *is wheeling in a huge wedding
cake, very fast.* AVON *is forced to retreat out of its line.*

SIDNEY. Everybody *scream.*

A band follows SIDNEY *and the cake. They are playing a fast
version of 'Bye Bye Blackbird'. The cake has 'LUCY' written
on it with a heart and a huge dripping red arrow.*
SIDNEY *has a four-foot cardboard knife. He and* LUCY *help
up* BAGLEY, *manoeuvre him into place to cut the cake.*

SIDNEY. Cut the cake, Uncle. Fruity slabs all round.

LUCY. Come on, Uncle.
BAGLEY (*lifting the huge knife like a maniac*). I'll carve.

> BAGLEY *holds the knife up above the cake.* BASSETT *has a flash of insight.*

BASSETT. He pushed that woman down the air-raid shelter steps.

> *The knife descends. The cake opens and out comes a* TAP-DANCER *in period strip tassles, with red heart motifs. In each hand she carries one foot high wedding symbols: a little man in a top hat and a little woman in wedding dress. The* TAP-DANCER *dances on the table. A minute's superb dancing.*

RODERICK. Sidney!
SIDNEY (*laughing*). Lucy!
RODERICK. Your bloody sense of humour.
VANESSA. Roderick –

> EDMUNDS *reaches his hand up the* TAPDANCER'S *thigh.*

EDMUNDS. Second course.
BASSETT. Nice bit of lamb.
ROCHESTER. Wrapped up in a gymslip.

> *Virtuoso tap. Much applauded.* EDMUNDS *grabs occasionally.* BAGLEY *is still in a small huddle with* LUCY. *Then he breaks away from her and lifts the great knife.*

LUCY. No, Uncle, No.

> BAGLEY *slams it down on the table with a great cry.*

BAGLEY. BOAZ.

> *The table breaks in two, cascading plates and cutlery. The* DANCER *leaps clear.* BAGLEY *goes under, inert. The band grinds to a halt.*

LUCY. Oh, Christ. (*She scrabbles among the debris.*)

RODERICK. Majordomo, clear the room.

MAJORDOMO. Of course, Mr Bagley. Could we . . . (*He seizes up.*)

RODERICK. Get out of here, you little tart.

The TAPDANCER *runs off crying.*

LUCY. He's dead. There's something coming out of his nose.

SIDNEY *has rushed over.*

VANESSA. We need a doctor.

LUCY. He's dead. (LUCY *moves away as* SIDNEY *moves in on the body.*)

VANESSA. Dear God, help us all, he's gone.

RODERICK. Don't go too close.

ROCHESTER. Shall I . . .

A scene of activity. Only LUCY *has broken away from the main body. Everyone else moves about, shocked.*

VANESSA. Shouldn't we close his eyes?

The curtain begins to fall slowly.

CLIVE. Died with a very funny look.

EDMUNDS. 'S great man. 'S great man.

VANESSA. God. Oh God.

CLIVE. Horrible.

BASSETT. My God, if that was the wedding what the hell will they do for the funeral?

LUCY. I wanna divorce. I wanna divorce.

The curtain falls.

ACT TWO

A country scene. Some bushes.
Bright sunlight. Birdsong.
The sound of a hunting horn.
RODERICK BAGLEY *gallops across the stage on a horse. He is in*
hunting dress. He is now 58.

Pause.

The sound of a hunting horn and hounds. Silence. From behind a
bush JAMES AVON, *now 66, stands up unsteadily. He is physically*
transformed from the previous act.
He stands furtively behind the bush and looks about.
He takes out a hip-flask and drinks long and deep.
LUCY BAGLEY, *now 35 and radiantly beautiful, walks on in hunt-*
ing dress and with a riding crop.
They stare at each other.

AVON. I'm sorry . . . I fell.

> *Pause.*

> Here. Half an hour ago. I'm glad the day . . . (*He gestures.*
A pause.)
> Follow the hunt.

> *He retreats off the stage. A pause.* LUCY *yawns luxuriantly,*
then slaps her riding crop on her thigh twice.
> CLIVE AVON *comes on in riding dress.*

LUCY. Your father was lying down over there.

CLIVE. Ah.

LUCY. Shouldn't you play the dutiful son?

CLIVE. As long as he didn't have a bottle. He didn't have a bottle, did he?

LUCY *smiles and shrugs*.

CLIVE. That's all right then. (*Pause.*) 'ello, Lucy.

LUCY. Why 'ello, Clive.

Pause.

CLIVE. Haven't seen your father this morning.

LUCY. He went through this hollow five minutes ago.

CLIVE. Going well?

LUCY. What do you think?

CLIVE. I think the Master of the Stanton Vale Hunt was almost certainly going well. Did you . . . fall off?

LUCY. I got bored. So I sent Fanlight home. I thought I'd wander about a bit. So. I'm wandering about.

CLIVE. Yes?

LUCY. Yes.

CLIVE (*backs away*). I'd better take a look at Dad.

LUCY. You know he's all right. Let him be.

CLIVE. All the same . . .

LUCY. Let him lie. I'm all for people finding what pleasure they can. (*Pause.*) Stick your tongue out.

CLIVE. Lucy.

LUCY. Stick your tongue out. I want to see your tongue. How pink it is.

CLIVE. Lucy, no.

LUCY. Please. You look a bit under the weather. A bit peaky. If your tongue's furry . . . you're peaky.

CLIVE. No.

LUCY. Pleeeease . . .

CLIVE. Lucy. Not in the open air again.

A long pause.

LUCY. You can stick your tongue out in the open air.

CLIVE. I've been dreading this meet, Lucy. The last meet of the season. After what happened last year. On the last meet of the season. I . . . bit squeamish.

LUCY. You said . . . I love your body in this light.

CLIVE. Yes.

LUCY. Yes.

CLIVE. That sounds like me. Squeamish. Like . . .

LUCY. I love your body . . .

CLIVE. Like your three husbands.

Pause.

LUCY. 'Show me the tongue that once upon a time . . .' That's a line from one of my Mum's poems. *Stanton Garden* by Vanessa Bagley. 'Show me the tongue that once upon a time licked and slobbered . . .' (*Pause.*) Doesn't actually go on like that.

CLIVE. I don't really want to go through . . . it all again.

LUCY. You already are.

CLIVE. This time, Lucy, please, no . . . sort of . . .

LUCY. As you say . . .

CLIVE. No . . . I was . . . know exactly what I'm doing. That's the worst thing about it. I know exactly what I'm doing.

LUCY. Isn't the worst thing that you like what you know that you're doing?

CLIVE. Yes.

LUCY. We'll read about it in the paper. 'At the 1969 Stanton Vale Spring Meet sexual intercourse was enjoyed by Miss Lucy Bagley, formerly Mrs Ralph du Sautoy, formerly Mrs Leonard Fitzgibbon, formerly Mrs Dennis Macpherson . . . and Mr Clive Avon.'

CLIVE. All right.

LUCY. Yes?

CLIVE. Yes.

LUCY. Lovely.
CLIVE. Yes . . . if nobody speaks.
LUCY. Fine.
CLIVE. No words.
LUCY. Fine.

Pause. They start to go.

Give me a cuddle.
CLIVE. Please.

LUCY at once puts her fingers to her lips. They go silently behind the bush.
Pause. Then from off.

EDMUNDS (*off*). Over 'ere for a smoke, boys.

Enter EDMUNDS, now obscenely large, 64, red in the face. Followed by BASSETT, now 51. And ROCHESTER now 54.

EDMUNDS. 'Orse's breath. Smell of leather. Up above the country. Riding 'igh and all that. Dying for a fag.

AVON wanders on looking for a place to sit.

Oi. Oi.

At once EDMUNDS signals to BASSETT and ROCHESTER. They veer off in another direction to avoid meeting AVON. BASSETT mimes an elaborate yawn to show his contempt. AVON sits down and takes out a small black notebook. He speaks to himself.

AVON. Ladies' night.
EDMUNDS. Let's go over 'ere. (*They sit as far away from AVON as possible.*)
BASSETT. Look. Look. There he goes.
ROCHESTER. Who?
BASSETT. Look. Roderick. Up there on the hillside.
EDMUNDS. Look at him.

BASSETT. What a man.

EDMUNDS. It's easy on that 'orse. If I 'ad that 'orse I'd be up there.

ROCHESTER. 'Course you would, Harry.

EDMUNDS. 'Stead of down 'ere.

BASSETT (*of* AVON). He's got his little black book out.

EDMUNDS. The 'orse was given 'im. Of course.

BASSETT. Of course.

EDMUNDS. 'Ere comes Roderick's public relations man. Looking for somebody whose day 'e can ruin.

> EDMUNDS *smiles at* BROWNE *as he enters, not in hunting gear, but uneasy country mix. He looks like an estate manager.*

'Allo, Tom.

> BASSETT, ROCHESTER *and* EDMUNDS *huddle like guilty schoolboys.*

BROWNE. Is somebody fixing Roderick's lunch?

BASSETT. Dunno.

EDMUNDS. Dunno.

ROCHESTER. Should think so.

BROWNE. Roderick's going to be very hungry, you know. After such a terrific ride. He's fairly galloping. I've had to make arrangements over twenty miles. I've had the idea of walky-talkies next year. And a helicopter. Get me from here to Transport House. Excellent. Excellent. (BROWNE *goes out.*)

EDMUNDS. Oh, Tom . . . (*But* BROWNE's *gone.* EDMUNDS *gives a 'V'*.) I remember 'im when 'e was a little Commie 'ot 'ead.

ROCHESTER. Now risen without trace.

EDMUNDS. Like so many.

BASSETT. Aren't walky-talkies illegal anyway?

EDMUNDS. Am I going soft, Bill . . .

ROCHESTER. Mmmmm . . .

EDMUNDS. Because I find that man deeply offensive. People should be one thing or another. You can't work for Roderick

Bagley and be big wheel in Transport House. I mean what does Tom believe? Rod's a right-wing Tory . . .

ROCHESTER. It's all public relations . . .

EDMUNDS. How does Tom do it? In his mind? Is it bow tie and dicky for Roderick? And a baggy old suit for Transport House? I mean, what does Roderick feel? Working with a man 'oo's blatantly Labour . . .

ROCHESTER. They're both intelligent men . . .

EDMUNDS. And what does that mean?

ROCHESTER. Well . . . you know how it is.

BASSETT. Oh aye.

EDMUNDS. Oh aye.

ROCHESTER. Hallo, Jimmy. All right?

AVON *waves his book.*

AVON. Ladies' night.

ROCHESTER. Yes. Jimmy. Yes. All right?

AVON *nods and smiles.* BASSETT, *grinning, speaks under his breath.*

BASSETT. Just stay where you are, Jimmy.

EDMUNDS. Tail wags dog, if you ask me. Tom Browne runs Roderick Bagley.

ROCHESTER. It's . . . more complex.

EDMUNDS. I mean, 'ow does it work? 'Ow can they see eye to eye?

ROCHESTER. I don't think you're getting soft, Harry. Just a little loose at the mouth.

BASSETT. Good old Rod. We've all done well.

ROCHESTER. There goes Roderick.

EDMUNDS. Where?

BASSETT. Hillside. Going the other way now.

EDMUNDS. Yes.

BASSETT. We've all done well. Thank you, Gov.

Enter VANESSA, *now 57. Headscarf. Sensible shoes.*

VANESSA. Hallo, everyone.

ROCHESTER. Mrs Bagley.

VANESSA. Please don't anyone get up for me.

    EDMUNDS *smiles.*

EDMUNDS. Mph.

BASSETT. A perfectly contented man.

VANESSA. I was meant to be meeting Roderick.

EDMUNDS. Tom's 'ad to make arrangements over twenty miles.

VANESSA. Gosh. Poor Tom.

ROCHESTER. Poor Tom.

AVON. Ah Mrs Bagley. I've been wanting to ask you . . .

    VANESSA *goes over to* AVON.

VANESSA. Hello, James.

AVON. I'm just compiling the list for Ladies' night at the Masonic
Lodge. Roderick allocated me . . . for the job.

EDMUNDS. The arable land. Roderick's arable land round 'ere.

    (EDMUNDS *goes out, frowning.*)

VANESSA. Ah yes.

AVON. Will you be coming this year?

VANESSA. Well . . .

AVON. I'd like to put you down on my list.

VANESSA. Yes. It's just . . . surely . . . surely it's eight months
away.

AVON. Yes, yes. (*Pause.*) Get it sorted out. I'm in charge of it,
you know.

    SIDNEY *comes on, now 36. Sharp city dress. With him is*
    RAYMOND FINCH, *53. We do not know who he is.*

SIDNEY. Ah, mother. I think we're all meant to be meeting for
lunch.

VANESSA. Oh dear.

AVON. Get it sorted out.

SIDNEY. Hasn't Tom fixed it?

BASSETT. He was here a minute ago. Rubbed me lamp and up he popped. Public Relations.

SIDNEY. We have guests. (SIDNEY *turns to* FINCH *who is looking very lost.*) I particularly wanted you to meet my brother Martin. He's very much the . . . dynamic young man.

VANESSA. Martin is here. Somewhere.

Enter TOM BROWNE *with a pile of books.*

BROWNE. Ah, Raymond. Here are the books, Vanessa.

VANESSA. Thank you, Tom.

SIDNEY. We were wondering, Tom, about a spot of lunch.

BROWNE. I've just ordered lunch in Milton Bassett. At the Crop and Saddle. But if you want a picnic, no problem. (BROWNE *smiles at* FINCH *to impress.*) I'm sure I can fix it.

FINCH. Country pursuits, Tom?

BROWNE. Oh yes.

SIDNEY. Good.

BROWNE. I'll go down to that farm. See what the farmer's wife has got. In her larder. In her fridge. Bound to have something. Give her some money.

SIDNEY. All right.

BROWNE. Just whatever's handy.

Pause. BROWNE *looks at* FINCH.

SIDNEY. Fine.

BROWNE. I'll tell her it's for the Bagleys.

SIDNEY. Fine.

BROWNE *goes out.* VANESSA *is sorting out a pile of books on the ground.*

VANESSA. I want to give you all a book.

Pause. No one has heard.

I'd like to give you all a book of my poems.

ROCHESTER. I see.

VANESSA. Of my poems.

BASSETT. Ah.

ROCHESTER. I see. Very . . .

VANESSA. My first published collection. *Flowers From A Stanton Garden.* Each poem is a flower, you see.

ROCHESTER. I see. Very . . .

VANESSA. The collection opens with some slight, occasional pieces . . . small gentle poems. Pansy. Primrose. And Winter Crocus. But we're pretty soon into the Hollihocks and the Giant Dahlias.

SIDNEY. Mother –

VANESSA. Yes, dear?

SIDNEY. Do you think Tom's all right on his own? I'll just see how he's coping.

SIDNEY *goes out.* VANESSA *has opened a copy.*

VANESSA. Shall I . . .

BASSETT. Ah.

VANESSA. 'Stanton sleeps. The milkman calls.
      The housewife and the worker wake.
      The children trot to dreary schools.
      We only skim, as birds upon a lake.

      Turning perhaps through some domestic task,
      We catch the casual mirror in our eye.
      As over rooves and Stanton chimneys stark
      We see the vivid, all-embracing sky.

      How many secrets are concealed
      How many tragic lives are led
      Behind the shutters of Stanton's doors
      Stanton's living becoming Stanton's dead.'

Pause.

ROCHESTER. Pansy?

VANESSA. Geranium.

ROCHESTER. A bitter flower.

VANESSA. Yes, that is the import of the poem. (VANESSA *hands a copy to* BASSETT.) There you are.

BASSETT. Thank you. Prop up leg o' kitchen table.

VANESSA. What? Oh yes.

BASSETT. No, it's charming, charming.

VANESSA (*to* FINCH, *who is embarrassed*). Oh, good afternoon. You're a friend of Sidney's?

FINCH. Yes.

VANESSA. I'm Sidney's mother. Would you like one?

> CLIVE *rises, fully clothed, from behind the bushes.* FINCH *sees him. They catch each other's eye.* CLIVE *goes off fast.*

Mr . . .?

FINCH. Finch. Finch. (*He takes a book.*) Thank you.

> *All have got books. They all glance inside them.* VANESSA *sighs.*

VANESSA. Well, there we are.

> MARTIN *comes on. Now 33. Very soft.*

MARTIN. Mr Finch? Sidney sent me up.

FINCH. Ah you must be Martin Bagley.

> MARTIN *thinks.*

MARTIN. Yes, I'm Sidney's brother.

FINCH. How do you do. Your brother told me about you.

MARTIN. Oh . . . dear. What did he say?

FINCH. He said you were the coming man.

MARTIN. Yes. Yes. Yes . . . I . . . Yes. I am.

VANESSA. It's such a pity the sticky buds have got so far on before I thought. (VANESSA *wanders out.*)

MARTIN. I'm going to work on the Hong Kong side now.
FINCH. I think you'll find everything very satisfactory out there.
MARTIN. You had a good trip?
FINCH. Oh yes. I fixed the contract for the Broiler Hen Combine.

MARTIN *and* FINCH *begin to stroll off.*

MARTIN. Oh good.
FINCH. Crowded island, Hong Kong.
MARTIN. Yes. We found ourselves in eggs.

As they go off, EDMUNDS *meets them. He becomes ingratiating.*

EDMUNDS. Oh. Oh. 'Allo, Ray. Nice to see you up 'ere. (*They shake.*)
FINCH. Hello, Harry.
EDMUNDS (*laughs*). On my patch, eh?

MARTIN *and* FINCH *go out.* EDMUNDS *walks quickly over to* ROCHESTER *and* BASSETT.

That's a bit ripe, Bill.
ROCHESTER. What?
EDMUNDS. That's bloody ripe. A Tory ex-Government Minister on my patch.
ROCHESTER. Ah.

Pause.

EDMUNDS. Raymond Finch. You did know it was Finch?
ROCHESTER. Yes. I know it was Finch.
EDMUNDS. You did know 'e was coming?
ROCHESTER. Not directly.
EDMUNDS. But you're the Bagley lawyer. You're meant to know everything round 'ere.
ROCHESTER. All right. All right. So I didn't connect.
EDMUNDS. What were they talking about?
ROCHESTER. Oh, come on.
BASSETT. Hong Kong, wasn't it, Bill?

EDMUNDS. 'Ong Kong? When's 'e going?

BASSETT. From what I heard he's been.

A pause. EDMUNDS *moves away.*

Harry, there's steam coming out of your ears.

EDMUNDS. I were going to 'Ong Kong. Next month's Labour Delegation.

BASSETT. Doing a little Bagley Business on the side?

EDMUNDS. Roderick knows I'm 'is man in Asia. Always 'ave been. You telling me 'e's 'ad Finch do it? Not me? (*Pause.*) An ex-Minister?

Pause. ROCHESTER *just stares.*

My sleeves 'ave been rolled up for thirty years. In spite of everything, against the grain of 'aving to provide. In there with the best of them, slamming up houses, motorways, 'ospitals, swimming pools, mobilizing funds and spreading loads. I've worked with 'em all. Dicky Councillors, fixers, pushers, old family firms, political wild boys saying I'm no socialist, and Old Etonian ministers crapping on about Maynard Keynes. I've dragged myself down among 'em, knuckled, elbowed, pushed and shoved, jostled in the speculative mêlée, I'll work with anyone to do good for the people of this country. I'm willing to work alongside any man. I'm even willing to work for Roderick Bagley, God Almighty 'Imself. But we must let each other know what we're doing!

He never told me.

Do we know what we're doing? Does Bagley know what 'e's doing? Look at this land 'e owns. 'E's an architect, not a farmer. 'E's not even an Architect. 'E's not qualified, and 'e's building a factory in 'Ong Kong. For chickens. Well who is 'e? In 'Ong Kong. Does 'e run 'Ong Kong Town Council or something? (*Change.*) It's all been a Bagley mystery tour. We're all on this bus. Tickets taken away. Door locked. And it may be Blackpool. Or Morecambe. Or Scarborough. (*Pause.*)

Or the finest 'Otel Complex north of a line between the Severn and the Wash. (*Pause.*) Or the biggest Arts Centre this side of the Pennines, or that side of the Pennines . . . (*Pause.*) Or the fourth new London Airport on the banks of the 'Umber. (*Pause.*) Or shall we all die . . . Crushed to death in one of 'is jerry-built underground car parks?

Long pause. Then ROCHESTER, *dead quiet.*

ROCHESTER. Shut up, Harry.

EDMUNDS. Didn't want to go to 'Ong Kong anyway. (*A pause.* EDMUNDS *walks away.*) Do you think . . . Maybe Ray . . . Didn't . . . I could ask Roderick . . . Some ends to tie up When I'm in 'Ong Kong?

AVON *has just woken up. He opens his book.*

AVON. Embossed invitations?

Enter MARTIN *and* FINCH. *They have wheeled round on their walk.*

MARTIN. So that's all right for you, then. On the twelfth.

FINCH (*to* EDMUNDS). Ah Harry, been talking to Martin here. Bagleys want me to cover Africa, as well as Asia.

EDMUNDS *just stares. At once a farmer's* BOY *comes on carrying two buckets.*

BOY. Are you . . . The people . . . ?

BROWNE *sweeps on behind him.*

BROWNE. Thank you, lad. (*To* FINCH.) No trouble there. Do you know everyone? (BROWNE *shakes* FINCH's *hand.*)

FINCH. Cleaned out the farmer's larder?

BROWNE. Do you know Bill Rochester?

ROCHESTER. We did meet once.

FINCH. Yes. Yes. Of course. How's . . .

ROCHESTER. Very well.

BROWNE. Bill does all our legal work. At this level.
FINCH. Of course.

   BASSETT *steps forward confidently.*

BASSETT. How are you?
BROWNE. Duncan Bassett. Brewer.
BASSETT. A local. Admired you for a long time.

   SIDNEY *has come on and is now giving the* BOY *a tip.* SIDNEY
   upturns the buckets on a cloth he has laid.

SIDNEY. Riot and excess.
BROWNE. And you do know Harry.
EDMUNDS. Of old.
BROWNE. And I would particularly like you to meet Martin
   Bagley, the youngest.

   The BOY *is passing.* BROWNE *stops him as he goes.*

   How much did he give you, lad?
MARTIN. I don't think Tom realizes . . .
BOY. A pound.
BROWNE. That's OK.

   The BOY *goes off.*

   What didn't I realize?
FINCH. I've been talking to Martin about going to Africa.

   EDMUNDS *is helping* SIDNEY *with the picnic.*

EDMUNDS. Frozen peas.
BROWNE. Ah. Using your initiative, Martin. Roderick's just
   moved Martin to Foreign Contracts, after giving him a try on
   Subsidiary Civic Amenities. Cricket Pavilions, that sort of
   thing. Is that not right, Martin? Or did that come before Farm
   Management? And your short spell in air-vents.
MARTIN. I'm interested in the research side.
EDMUNDS. Frozen solid.

BROWNE. His father keeps him busy.

MARTIN. I've written a report on the research side. Its called a Report on Research.

   EDMUNDS *lays the peas on the ground, downstage.*

EDMUNDS. They'll be all right here. Sun should warm them.

MARTIN. Three hundred pages.

BROWNE. I'll let you have a summary, Raymond. Couple of sides. Now really, about Africa. Roderick. And you. (BROWNE *leads* FINCH *off.*)

MARTIN (*to* BASSETT). Do you think I did the right thing? Talking to Mr Finch?

BASSETT. Non-committally, Martin, you did . . . Or did not . . . Do the right thing. But don't quote me.

MARTIN. No. I'm at night school, you know. Business and politics.

EDMUNDS. Don't tread on my peas.

MARTIN. No. (MARTIN *walks away.*)

BASSETT. Jesus wept.

   SIDNEY *has laid the picnic out. He sits back.*

SIDNEY. Lunch, everybody.

   BROWNE *and* FINCH *enter.*

BROWNE. Eight percent. Commission, but we're going to keep that tight in our fist.

FINCH. Quite right.

BROWNE. Means more for you. Ah, food. (BROWNE *bellows formally.*) Everybody in the area, come for lunch. Now.

   SIDNEY *sits apart and starts elaborately rolling a joint.* VANESSA *comes in.* CLIVE *goes to his father and takes his flask. Kisses his cheek.*

FINCH. I know it's the point not to ask at all, but surely we could ask for nine. After all, the Chinese asked for ten.

BROWNE. Play it by ear.

BASSETT. Did I see some drink?

CLIVE *silently hands him the flask.*

BROWNE. Ham. Pickle. Nothing to cut with.

SIDNEY *takes a flick knife out of the breast pocket of his pinstripe suit.*

SIDNEY. Shazzam. (*He flicks the knife open and throws it into the ham. They all stare.*)

BROWNE. The farmer's wife's given us plates and cups and lime cordial. (BROWNE *fingers out an oblong on the ground.*) If this is the table, Ray, you sit at the top as our honoured guest. And this is Clive Avon, Raymond Finch.

CLIVE *sits down without a word. The meal begins.*

FINCH. It's a wonderful . . . Chance for me. Get away at week-ends, do something completely different. Sit about in the open air. Get away from the hothouse. One's concerns get so easily confined in Westminster. Is that Piccalilli? It's good to go out and be reminded there's a world North of Watford.

Pause.

CLIVE. Raymond Finch. Tory ex-Minister.

FINCH *smiles.*

Longtime Junior in Colonial Office. Sometime Senior in Ministry of Housing. When out of office will offer Governmental expertise in Private Industry. Keeps his skills greased. Will offer them around. A worthy man, a worthwhile man to have on the notepaper. Slipping in and out of Government to lend out a face everybody knows they know. A respectable man, respected, a blazer for other men to wear. Ministers available, cut out the form at the back of the investor's chronicle. Now Roderick Bagley's accredited Representative, well paid, a man for all notepaper. What kind of man was this?

Pause.

Vaseline man.

Everyone has stopped eating. FINCH *reaches for the chutney. Everyone watches him.* FINCH *keeping cool.*

ROCHESTER. The early days of the Industrial Revolution must have been very beautiful indeed. To climb over a hill and to look into the valley where you saw, perhaps, one minehead . . . With those beautiful iron props . . . And just a few rows of houses. I'm sure the countryside looked better for it originally. The black against the wheat. (*Pause. To* BASSETT.) What do you say?

CLIVE. Vaseline. The stuff buggers use.

Pause.

ROCHESTER. Always beer . . . Was it . . . With you . . . Duncan?

BASSETT. Always brewing. Threw me in a barrel at eighteen months. Tell you. I were up the University the other night . . .

ROCHESTER (*smiles*). The new University . . .

BASSETT. Stanton University. I've got the catering contract there . . .

ROCHESTER. Yes.

BASSETT. Well, as Bagley built it . . .

ROCHESTER. Yes.

BASSETT. I got the contract . . . Like I do. (*Pause.*) Wherever . . . (*Pause.*) Bagley . . .

CLIVE. Builds?

Pause.

BASSETT. Up the University there were a boy that night who'd never tasted beer before. At the age of nineteen. I gave 'im a free bottle. 'Sup this,' I said. Bassett's Ale. He drank it down. His first ever glass of ale. Then he looked at me and he said . . . 'I expect old men like you to piss on the workers. But kindly don't piss on the workers in bottles.'

Long pause. SIDNEY *has finished his joint and now walks out.*
BASSETT *laughs to cheer the others. Fails.*

Eh? What about that? Eh?

CLIVE. Pin stripe slime running our lives. Why should we expect
any better?

BROWNE. Than what, Clive? Better than what? If you want to
be childishly, pointlessly rude to Mr Finch . . . to Raymond . . .
Then let's have it, let's hear it, let's consider it, let's weight it
for what it is, and let's hang it out to dry, so we can all enjoy
our ham.

Pause.

FINCH. Thank you, Tom.

BROWNE. And if you have nothing to say, and only a little all-
purpose spite, then I think it would be best all round if you
would go.

CLIVE *gets up and goes out at once.*

BROWNE. I do think it best to cut things off, to cut people off
when they go like that. Cauterize. Why not?

VANESSA. I need a rhyme for 'sunlit valley'.

BROWNE. I don't see why we should have to listen to ill-informed
criticism which is only abuse. Do you, Raymond? Decayed free
speech.

VANESSA *goes out.*

You do get used to it . . . I handle all Roderick's public relations . . . And I get a little tired of all the shit I have to
shovel from the door. Endless carping criticism because people
are envious of Rod's achievements. Well, you know, Raymond,
because you're in Parliament, that it's our common lot to be
subjected to petty abuse. But I don't think people realize the
amount of good we do. I've had to say this to three Cabinet
Ministers on both sides of the floor.

FINCH. Yes. Yes. I see what you mean. How did they react?

BROWNE. Just like you, Ray.

FINCH. Yes. Yes.

MARTIN (*excited*). Aunty Sally.

BROWNE. What?

MARTIN. Mother's rhyme. 'Sunlit Valley' . . . 'Aunty Sally'.

Enter CLIVE *very fast. He is carrying in his hand a huge dollop of horse dung.*

EDMUNDS. Look out!

CLIVE *rams the horse dung down the back of* FINCH's *neck.*

BROWNE. Oh, for God's sake.

BASSETT. What is it, what is it?

BROWNE. My God, how stupid.

ROCHESTER. How utterly pathetic.

CLIVE *backs away upstage. They ignore him.*

BASSETT. What is it?

EDMUNDS. 'Orse . . .

ROCHESTER. Dung.

BROWNE. Manure.

EDMUNDS. . . . shit.

FINCH *is quietly taking off his jacket.*

BROWNE. Of all the bloody utterly pointless damn stupid things to do . . .

BASSETT. Bit silly.

MARTIN. Is it on your shirt?

FINCH. Don't worry. It's only m . . . muck. Don't panic.

BROWNE. I just wonder at the mind . . .

FINCH. Don't worry.

MARTIN. It is on your shirt.

BROWNE. Ray, I hope this hasn't upset you. Of course it has upset us all.

FINCH. No.

BROWNE. If Roderick had been here nothing like this could have got under way.

EDMUNDS (*quietly to* FINCH). Let me give you a 'and, playmate.

EDMUNDS *helps* FINCH *to take off his shirt.*)

BROWNE. I'm going to go too far. I know I'm going to go too far, but sometimes . . . working for Roderick is a right bastard.

EDMUNDS. Still –

BROWNE. Directly because of the people he's had to mix with. Local personalities, small men, egged on by minor members of the family. Men who once enjoyed some peripheral function, but who are just weeds under the shadow of the great oak tree that Roderick has become. Roderick knows about you all. You don't realize how big Roderick is. Sniggering behind your hands. There is simply no reason why an international business concern should be pestered by the bitcheries of a local hunt, even if Roderick is the Master. If Roderick has one fault . . . (*He turns ironically to* FINCH.) He is too kind-hearted. He suffers improprieties around him. People who can't keep their bodies under control. Decadence.

FINCH. I'm cold.

MARTIN. He's cold.

BASSETT, EDMUNDS, ROCHESTER, MARTIN *and* BROWNE *all take their jackets off.* FINCH *looks from one jacket to another.*

BROWNE. Will this incident affect your attitude in any way?

FINCH (*in a moment of incredible fury*). JESUS CHRIST.

Shocked silence.

I really think I must have a hot bath and a new suit of clothes.

BROWNE *puts his jacket on* FINCH's *shoulders. The others are left holding theirs.*

MARTIN. Farmhouse. The farmer's bath . . .

BROWNE. Good. Right. OK. Certainly. Let's go. Eh, Ray? We've had the food and now we'll get the bath. Good. Right. OK.

MARTIN. Was that a good idea?

BROWNE. OK, Ray?

FINCH. I don't know. I hope so.

BROWNE. Try the patience of a saint.

FINCH. Yes.

> MARTIN *is holding* FINCH's *befouled shirt and jacket.* MARTIN, FINCH *and* BROWNE *turn to go.* CLIVE *suddenly speaks from upstage.*

CLIVE. Look, I'm sorry. I'm very sorry. It was a stupid thing to do. I apologize and I'm very sorry.

> BROWNE *points at* CLIVE *a long time.* CLIVE *freezes* BROWNE *turns to* FINCH.

BROWNE. I don't want what's happened . . .

FINCH. No.

BROWNE. Will it?

> *They go off.* MARTIN *follows.* LUCY's *voice from behind the bush.*

LUCY. Why apologize? Why bloody apologize?

> BASSETT, EDMUNDS *and* ROCHESTER *turn round and put on jackets.* CLIVE *stares, then turns away and sits down.*

EDMUNDS. Well . . .

ROCHESTER. Well . . .

BASSETT. Well, well.

ROCHESTER. I wish . . . just occasionally . . . it was me . . . in the middle of one of those wonderful rows. I could dish it out . . .

EDMUNDS. But could you take it?

ROCHESTER. Well . . .

BASSETT. Can destroy a man.

EDMUNDS. What do you mean?

BASSETT. I have seen men destroyed. That's all.

EDMUNDS. My peas. My peas 'ave melted. Shall we 'ave 'em? Like a salad.

Enter SIDNEY.

SIDNEY. Coming down a meadow. My brother bearing dirty clothes. My father's public relations man gushing like a gas leak. Both in pursuit of a senior politician. Stripped to the waist and shaking his head. (*Pause.*) Missed something, did I?

EDMUNDS. Clive Avon stuffed shit down Finch's neck.

ROCHESTER. There was a slight hiatus.

BASSETT. Browne insulted local personalities.

EDMUNDS. It was really about Africa.

ROCHESTER. I think the hard ride took it out of everybody.

BASSETT. This one's going to fester.

SIDNEY. Ah. That's what happened.

LUCY *rises at the back from behind the bush.*

LUCY. Clive started something which he doesn't know how to finish. For the second time today. (LUCY *throws his tie over to* CLIVE.)

SIDNEY. Something wrong with him? Bit missing?

LUCY. Oh, Clive. Every word you said about Finch is true. He's all the things you say. And worse. A three-legged dog with just enough go. We know that. And Daddy knows that. So what?

SIDNEY. Did he make some kind of moral judgement?

LUCY. A little stutter of a judgement.

CLIVE. I . . .

LUCY. You stutter. (*Pause.*) Stutter. (*Pause.*) A little spurt.

SIDNEY. Did he expand his theme to include the whole Bagley family?

LUCY. He did.

SIDNEY. And how did we emerge?

LUCY. As brothelkeepers.

CLIVE. I apologized, Sidney . . .

SIDNEY. Shut up. I'm talking to my sister. Sister, were our interests damaged?

LUCY. Flesh wounds.

SIDNEY. No blood.

LUCY. No blood.

Pause.

BASSETT. Well, as the picnic's a bit . . . trampled on . . . I think we should . . . be moving off.

ROCHESTER. Showers at the Club.

BASSETT. A good soap.

SIDNEY *turns.*

SIDNEY. I think Roderick would prefer you to stay. For the hanging. In my father's absence I assume command.

BASSETT *makes to go.*

EDMUNDS (*sharply*). Sit down.

SIDNEY. I don't share my father's enthusiasm for the Bagley empire. I can't get worked up. I don't believe in it. I just believe it exists. I prefer London life . . . moving between the city and my firm of Leisure Amenities. Collecting the cheque from the Amusement Arcade and going back home. Or to dip my wick in a dirty cup.

LUCY. Listen to this, Clive.

SIDNEY. Yes, listen. Three-quarters of the business is public relations. Tom Browne. Public relations means fixing contracts, arranging tenders, that sort of thing. A kind of banking. Human banking. Building up a pool of friends to be cashed at any branch. That's dreary work. I don't take any part in it.

And all those double scotches and double meanings. I hate double meanings. Hello when you mean Goodbye. Will you when you mean Don't you dare, You're Doing Very Well when you mean You're Dead. It's all good work for the Tom Brownes of this world but it gives me . . . no buzz at all. No thrill. So what's my tickle, Clive? Retribution.

CLIVE. You people are cruel and vicious.

SIDNEY. Basically we are a firm of architects. But yes.

SIDNEY *and* LUCY *move in on* CLIVE.

LUCY. It's coming, Clive.

BASSETT. There's going to be violence.

LUCY. Here it comes. Hold your tongue back in your mouth so you won't bite it off when we do it to you.

BASSETT. Oh my God.

LUCY. Now, Clive.

BASSETT *closes his eyes. He flinches.*

SIDNEY. Cardiff.

Long pause.

BASSETT. What happened?

CLIVE. You bastard.

SIDNEY. Cardiff.

CLIVE. Yes.

SIDNEY. The drainage contract.

CLIVE. Yes.

SIDNEY. The tender you are about to win.

CLIVE. Yes.

SIDNEY. You have lost. (*He clicks his fingers.*) Now.

CLIVE. Yes.

Pause. LUCY *kisses* CLIVE.

LUCY. How do you feel, Clive?

No reply.

How do you think he feels, Sid?

SIDNEY. Mature.

CLIVE walks off. SIDNEY has wandered a pace or two away.
LUCY lies down. SIDNEY quotes, dreamily.

'The young boy held it like a potato he was skinning in the
sink.'

EDMUNDS. That were totally unnecessary. Totally unnecessary.

SIDNEY. Where's my knife?

ROCHESTER. It's simply not true. That is not how your father's
business is run.

SIDNEY goes right up to ROCHESTER.

SIDNEY. Run. Run. Run? Not run? Not run like that? Browne
came up to me in that field. Said See to Clive now that Finch
has gone. I asked him How? Use Clive's drains in Cardiff
he said. I never heard of Cardiff. Nor of Clive's drains. Till
five minutes ago. And now I'll never think of them again.
Run, run. That's how. Q.E.D. My knife.

*EDMUNDS gets the knife out of his top pocket. He hands it to
SIDNEY with a thin smile.*

EDMUNDS. Just playing with it.

*SIDNEY takes the knife and goes upstage. He lies down with
his head in LUCY's lap. BASSETT glances at ROCHESTER.*

BASSETT. What's he doing?

ROCHESTER. He's lying down.

BASSETT. Is he asleep?

ROCHESTER. His eyes are closed. (*He looks away.*) No, they're
not.

BASSETT. Is he planning sleep?

ROCHESTER. I think so . . . if we just sit here . . . then choose
our moment.

BASSETT. Roger.

Everyone is quite still. Pause.

EDMUNDS. We 'ad a chance in 1945. Finest government this country ever 'ad. But not good enough. Not quite good enough by half. By the end, in rags. What am I now? I know. Don't answer that, 'Arry Edmunds. 'Ow can we ever forgive our-selves? I can't forgive myself. Labour party, the party we all love. (*Pause.*) Can we go 'ome now?

> CLIVE *has appeared.*

CLIVE. Dad, wake up.

AVON. You know that view, of the town . . . from the North-West . . . when you're on top of the hill . . . can you . . . see the public library from there? (*Sudden quiet panic.*) Clive. I'm drunk.

> MARTIN *has come in, looking as if he is going to be sick.*

MARTIN. Everybody. Finch has gone home. Finch has got the train home. (*Pause.*) Tom's on the phone. (*Pause.*) He had a phone call in the farmhouse. From father. (*Pause.*) Father's gone bankrupt. (*Pause.*) And Finch has gone home. (*Pause.*) Father's credit has been overextended by too rapid a pro-gramme of diversification. (*Pause.*) And he's gone bankrupt.

> MARTIN *starts to cry.* CLIVE *leads* AVON *across the stage and off.*

CLIVE. Come on, Dad. Let's go home.

> SIDNEY *leaps up.*

SIDNEY. Martin. Martin.
MARTIN. It's too . . . horrible.

> MARTIN *runs off.* VANESSA *enters quietly. She has not heard the news.*

ROCHESTER. Listen. Listen. Is the Official Receiver in yet?

> ROCHESTER *goes off.*

SIDNEY. Martin, Martin.

> SIDNEY *runs out.*

BASSETT. Documents.

> BASSETT *runs off.*

EDMUNDS. Oh, my God. Oh, my God, it's coming. It's coming all over me.

> EDMUNDS *runs off.* LUCY *whacks her thigh, then goes.* VANESSA *is left alone on the stage. Pause.*

VANESSA. 'Sunlit Valley.' (*Pause.*) Dog-rose.

'Possessed with human pomp and fine displays
Men lurch about this earth in tragic ways.
Men dream up splendid plans, that never tally:
For dinosaurs once ruled this sunlit valley.'

> *Blackout.*

> *Silence.*

ACT THREE

SCENE ONE

Music: The Rolling Stones sing 'You can't always get what you want.' Photographs. The words of the song are projected as they are sung, line by line, as follows:

'I saw her today at the reception
A glass of wine in her hand
I knew she would meet her connection
At her feet was a footloose man

'You can't always get what you want
You can't always get what you want
You can't always get what you want
But if you try sometime
You just might find
You get what you need'

Then photograph of modern office development, housing estates. Then drop in the Labour Club. High green windows. Big and airy. At the front a billiards table covered over and stacked with paper. LET'S GO WITH LABOUR *on the wall at the back.*
Lights up.

ROCHESTER *is sitting alone. Listening to the Rolling Stones.* SIDNEY *comes in. He turns up the radio to full blast and gets out a can of aerosol. Squirts it lavishly round the room.* ROCHESTER *turns the radio off.* SIDNEY *turns it on again.* ROCHESTER *pauses, turns the radio off. Pause.*

SIDNEY. To die . . . in the Labour club . . . of bankruptcy . . .

Enter RODERICK, *bland. He sits down.*

RODERICK. Bill . . .

ROCHESTER. Roderick . . .

SIDNEY. How was it in the dock today, Dad?

RODERICK. Fine. Usual stuff.

SIDNEY (*lightly*). Do they think you did it?

RODERICK. I'm not on trial. It's not a crime in this country. To have no money.

SIDNEY. No.

RODERICK. It's agonizing to confess every day in public that my profit margins were paper thin. It's dreadful having to go back, to re-invent my life. I try to be honest. Makes me look a fool.

SIDNEY. Or a saint.

RODERICK. People have been very kind. Like Harry lending us the Labour Club for our daily conflab. (*Pause.*) We ought to offer him something.

SIDNEY. The old leopard's spots shining, Dad . . .

RODERICK. Well, it wasn't all bad. Eh, Bill? (ROCHESTER *gets up at once and moves away.*) Bill? (*To* SIDNEY.) What's up with him?

SIDNEY. Nothing. Everyone . . . (*Change.*) Well, drinks then, is it? For the Leader of Her Majesty's Opposition.

RODERICK. Drinks. Yes. He'll expect drinks. Whisky.

SIDNEY. But Dad . . . We're bankrupt.

RODERICK. We are bankrupt. But that doesn't mean we're bankrupt.

SIDNEY. Subtle.

RODERICK. He won't be here for long. He's just changing trains and he won't want to be seen. He's made that very clear.

SIDNEY. Is he due?

ROCHESTER *is laying out papers on the table, not looking up.*

ROCHESTER. Now.

RODERICK. Very nice of him. Do you know, I like him.

ROCHESTER *turns away from the table.*

Thank you, Bill. (*Pause.*) I've asked for a carafe of water in the dock. But they still only give me a single glass. (*Pause.*) It's the little things, you know.

A noise from outside the room. They stand up at once. SIDNEY *pockets the aerosol.* RODERICK *straightens his tie.* ROCHESTER *takes the radio off the table. Pause. The door flies open.* BROWNE *storms in.* MARTIN *follows and quietly closes the door.*

BROWNE. You bloody idiot.

Pause.

SIDNEY. Where's the Leader?

BROWNE. On a train. Reading the evening paper. An inside page a long way down.

ROCHESTER. 'Bagley Admits He Gave Gifts!'

RODERICK. What do you mean?

BROWNE. Have you woken up to what you said in court today? You admitted you gave a bribe.

RODERICK. It was a gift.

BROWNE. A bribe of an estate wagon to a friend in the Ministry of Education. You damn well nearly named him . . . If you hadn't taken a sip of water, you would have named him.

RODERICK. That was nothing . . .

BROWNE. It was everything. It was graft. It was corruption. It was Chicago. When you said 'Gift' everyone in that court looked at you. And suddenly . . . You were a spiv. Because this morning you were a bankrupt. But tonight you're a fraud.

RODERICK. Fraud? I haven't lied, I haven't cheated . . .

ROCHESTER. For Christsake, fraud, fraud. Not moral fraud. Not not being a nice person. Real fraud. Criminal fraud. Fraud in

the eyes of the law. The Old Bailey. Black Marias. Editorials.
Wormwood Scrubs. Fraud. Fraud.

BROWNE. And that's what the man on the train's reading now.

Pause.

RODERICK. But the Counsel for the Creditors threatened me.
With some list he has . . . I had to say something.

BROWNE. What he actually said was: 'There is a list in my
possession of men in Public Office who have received remunera-
tion from your Companies for unstated services, including one
Minister Of The Crown.'

Everyone knew he meant Finch. You replied, Roderick: 'I
will see if I can find that list for the next hearing.'

SIDNEY. Christ, Dad.

BROWNE. A list. He said he had a list. Were you stupid enough
to keep a list? Was there a list with people on it you had
bought?

RODERICK. I don't know. I can't keep track of everything.

BROWNE. Was there a list?

Pause.

MARTIN. I kept a list. (*Pause.*) More a diary, actually. Times and
places. Meals. Observations. Insights. (MARTIN *reaches into
his briefcase and takes out a file.*) Here.

BROWNE *grabs the file. The papers fly into the air and they
all scramble to grab pages. They read.*

BROWNE. Jesus!

ROCHESTER. Oh my God.

SIDNEY. My Lamborghini.

BROWNE. Jesus.

RODERICK. Oh Martin, Martin, God forgive me.

MARTIN. The police have got the original. This is a photocopy.

ROCHESTER. It is. It's shiny. He's right.

BROWNE. Jesus.

MARTIN. I gave it to the police when they asked for it. I was documenting everything for the family history. When I write it.

BROWNE. The diary will go to the Director of Public Prosecutions. As sure as night follows day.

Pause.

RODERICK. Now, now, whose fault is this? Whose fault is it? Who should have known what Martin was doing?

ROCHESTER. Martin should have known what Martin was doing.

SIDNEY. There's no answer to that.

BROWNE. The diary will go to the Director of Public Prosecutions. As sure as night follows day.

Pause.

RODERICK. Somebody, somewhere . . . is gunning for us. An enemy of the family. And I don't know who it is. But who knows about us. Who now sits on a committee, or a board, somewhere, in London maybe. Who's got a vicious frame of mind. Somebody in the Establishment who detests everything I've tried to do, who doesn't like new methods, he's out to get me. Somebody who I've had lunch with, who has plotted anonymously, who has unearthed the evidence, who has talked to the police, who has shed the worst light possible, who has . . . who has . . . who has . . .

SIDNEY. Written Martin's diary for him?

RODERICK (*at full pitch*). God, I believe you all know him. I believe you all know who he is!

MARTIN. But Dad . . .

RODERICK. Shut up, you stupid, shambling boy.

SIDNEY. For Chrissake, Father. No one is getting at you. Nobody wants you. Your profit margins are not worth it. In the city they . . . You're a boil. You're burst. Nobody pricked you.

RODERICK. If we'd had more luck . . . The bad publicity from that ice rink . . . melting . . . because of the crack . . . in the structure.

SIDNEY. It's nothing to do with luck. It's to do with profit. We could have built in ice-cream as long as we made a profit.

RODERICK. If only we could pay the creditors.

ROCHESTER. With what? The force of your personality?

RODERICK. If only we could appeal to them. Or scare them off.

BROWNE. The Labour party will scare them off. Don't worry they will clear up the mess because of me. Because I'm their election campaign manager. Because I'm associated with you. Because I lent myself out to your organization. Because of the company I kept.

ROCHESTER. Crooks.

BROWNE. No. Incompetents. (*Pause.*) I will quote from my conversation with the Leader of Her Majesty's Opposition. 'A load of fucking bananas. Everybody run.' (*Close.*) The Labour Party will whisper down the line. Builders, councils, Government departments will gloss over fat bad debts . . . vast sums you owe will disappear in the fog. Books will be fiddled and invoices burnt the length of the land. Everyone will pay for the privilege of never having been publicly associated with a certain Midlands businessman. The bankruptcy case will vanish overnight so that everyone can sit back and enjoy the view. Of you. Skewered on the one isolated case of fraud.

SIDNEY. What a dazzling display of old-boys' knees-up. (*Pause.*) Pity somebody's got to go to jail.

They all look at RODERICK.

That's you, Dad. You will be the one token prosecution. Now that fraud has been mentioned. They'll pick on that one tiny obscure grotty little bribe, a long way from Westminster, that poor sod now innocently polishing the Volkswagen estate you bought him. That will do. Only one bribe has been mentioned. Therefore only one occurred. My poor Dad. Erased from the blackboard of public life. (*Pause.*)

RODERICK. Right, right. How do we get out of this one, Tom?

SIDNEY. Yes, come on, Tom. Public relations. Proposals A.B.C.D. Draft letters to friends. Dinner with Chief Constable. Sauna bath with a long lost cousin who became a judge.

> BROWNE *turns his briefcase upside down and papers fall out all over the floor.*

Oh come on, Tom. A.B.C.D. . . .

BROWNE. It's gone to the Fraud Squad. The Everest of public relations. The hardest one a PR man can ever be asked to crack. Local police . . . a little kindness. Judges . . . a little arselicking. Politicians . . . a little foreign travel. But the Fraud Squad. The Fraud Squad is outer space. They come from London in XJ12s, wearing oxygen masks. Their eyes are clear blue and when they see bad money they turn aquamarine.

SIDNEY. The little shit is running away.

BROWNE. You never understood it, did you, Rod? You never understood what your architect's practice had become. You were a sleepwalker. You never grasped – (*He searches for an example.*) Dear God, you never even grasped Employers National Insurance Contributions. Everyone was always years behind. I tried to explain. The little green stamp, Roderick . . . (*He makes squares with his fingers.*) In the little brown book.

We got top heavy. Too many buildings begun in too many places. And too much paid out in favours before a brick was laid. Too many hots laid in too many palms . . . And then . . . the world changed. National credit squeeze. The panic cheeseparing. Paying penalty clauses for the Bagley Pre-fab Stress System cracking in the rain. And the debts. Always the debts. Always having to pay out before we recouped. The frittering away. (*He is leaning over* RODERICK.) The unreality. God, I really want you to understand.

> Pause. Then RODERICK, *quiet, weary.*

RODERICK. All right. All right.

BROWNE (*cold and clear*). The day is coming when businesses will be run like high security prisons. No action that is not accounted, no gesture that is not cross-indexed, no indiscretion that is not costed and filed away. Piled up outside, cowboy architects and their families, bent politicians and wheeler-dealers, rotting on civic dumps, while inside their walls, teams of accountants roam the grounds with savage dogs, checking each door and the movement of executives from cell to cell. Not for punishment, but for profit. Every item will be valued, every job will be priced. We can't afford less if we're to go on. Making profits. (*He smiles.*) Great Britain Ltd. (*Pause.*) They're really going to go for you. (BROWNE *collects his briefcase and goes.*)

SIDNEY. The world walked out the door.

RODERICK. Right. OK. Let's look at this. (*Pause.*) Just the family. Looking at this. Stripped for action. (*His fist falls on the table.*) Pool our ideas. I will put something on the table. Vanessa has money.

SIDNEY. Oh no.

RODERICK. She is technically chairman of a small company which the receiver cannot touch. For I am bankrupt, not Vanessa. Now there is the possibility, and nobody speak please until they have turned this over in their minds, there is the possibility I could have Vanessa certified insane.

> *Pause.*

In all kindness. This is a strong possibility. Take her off the board and put Martin in.

MARTIN. I'm not going to do anything criminal, Dad.

RODERICK. It's not criminal, Martin. I just want some money. Now Bill, what is the law when a person who is chairman of a company . . . is certified . . . and incapable . . . if we were to certify her . . .

ROCHESTER. Roderick, if you want the money just ask Vanessa for it.

> *Pause.*

RODERICK. Ah. Yes.

ROCHESTER (*very slowly*). Just talk to her. Instead of putting
her in a mental asylum.

RODERICK. Too easy. We would be overheard.

Pause.

ROCHESTER. What . . . what do you want the money for?

RODERICK. To . . . (*A long pause.*) Diversify. (*Pause.*)

MARTIN. Karl Marx said, at night school . . .

Everyone looks at him but he persists.

Karl Marx said, there are contradictions inherent in a capitalist
system which in the end will destroy it. (*Pause.*) But I never
thought I'd see them in real life. (*Pause.*)

ROCHESTER. Don't talk that way about your father.

RODERICK. Perhaps the Judge will be a Freemason.

MARTIN *stands suddenly. Passion.*

MARTIN. You bloody lamed me. (*Pause.*) I was used. There was
dishonesty. At a personal level. I felt you got personal about me.
I was made to feel inferior. I was demeaned. Well . . . bugger.
Bugger it. And sod. I've smothered everything for you. My
loveliness. You've mutilated my . . . beauty. (*Pause.*) I'm
afraid father's made me cynical. And I'm going away. (*He goes
out leaving the door open.*)

Silence.

RODERICK. No. (*Pause.*) The tower block. In Burnley. When
the water ran down the living-room walls . . . of the people . . .
living there . . . and they got angry with me . . . and they threw
their refuse at me . . . how could I be expected to know . . . it
would rain . . . so hard . . . that winter?

EDMUNDS *folds into the open doorway.*

EDMUNDS. Sorry about this, Roderick. There's been a call.

Direct from very 'igh up. About you using Labour Club premises for your meetings. (*Pause.*) Could you not use Labour Club premises for your meetings? I liked 'aving you 'ere, but could you leave now . . .? (*Pause.*) If you went through back entrance you wouldn't 'ave to pass through dining-room. (*Pause.*) Sorry.

SIDNEY. Down we go.

The band strikes up. The Labour Club disappears. Music. Purple light. A FAN DANCER.

SCENE TWO

SIDNEY'S *plush strip club. 1973. Red velvet and champagne. A flashing sign: 'THE LOWER DEPTHS CLUB.'*
A strip act with fans is in progress.
Sitting at a table is DUNCAN BASSETT *with* LORD HARRY EDMUNDS. *At another, very small table is* TOM BROWNE. *He's not drinking.*
At another table there are LUCY AVON, CLIVE AVON *and* VANESSA BAGLEY. *They are stiff and silent.*
At another table there are several men.
The band riffs and the stripper's act finishes.

BANDLEADER. Take five.

ROCHESTER *enters in a dicky. Shifty now.*

ROCHESTER. 'Evening, Duncan, everything hunky dory? Hello, Harry.

EDMUNDS. Bill.

ROCHESTER. Nice to see you sipping at the fleshpots again.

EDMUNDS. I must say . . . Sidney's acts are getting very tasty.

ROCHESTER. Sidney knows his beetroot.

EDMUNDS. 'Is father . . .

ROCHESTER. Yes, Harry?

EDMUNDS. Got out today, didn't 'e. Remission. The whole family at the prison gate. I felt 'appier when there was a wall between 'im and me.

BASSETT. I must say, Harry, it's wonderful to see young Sidney back in Stanton again. After the tragedy. Making his way in the world. After all the humiliation. Starting his own place. Outfacing 'em all.

EDMUNDS. And 'is family.

BASSETT. Wonderful also, Harry.

EDMUNDS. 'Ave they looked at you? They 'aven't looked at me. Mind you, I 'aven't looked at them. 'Ow do you like working for a strip-club owner, Bill?

ROCHESTER. How do you like sitting in the House of Lords, Harry?

EDMUNDS. It's comfortable.

ROCHESTER. Likewise.

EDMUNDS. Marginally preferable to the ball and chain, which Roderick tried to clang round my leg. When 'e went berserk at that trial. Shouting names as they dragged 'im to 'is cell. Made *Who's Who* look like a bombsite. I was blown apart.

ROCHESTER. You didn't do badly. You made it to the Lords.

EDMUNDS. By the skin of my teeth. I 'ave to sit there grinning across at Finch. And all the other refugees from scandal and debauch.

ROCHESTER. We all have to flutter to the perch where we belong.

EDMUNDS. You've got philosophical. Since you went to seed.

ROCHESTER. What you up to, Tom?

BROWNE. I'm working again now. For charity. Champagne? I fiddle my expenses you know. (*He laughs.*)

EDMUNDS. We will all 'ave adjacent graves. All of us. After so many years and all the ups and downs, we are destined to rot in a row. I feel moved, if you get my drift.

The band strikes up. The lights narrow down to a spot. Kicking

*out from the side of the small stage a black-net-stockinged leg.
It grows and grows until it stretches to ten feet long.* SIDNEY
appears holding the leg.

SIDNEY. Thank you, dear. And dears.

> *The band stops. The lights come up.* SIDNEY *throws the leg
> aside. He speaks to the customers.*

All over. Club's closed. Private party.

MAN. But . . .

SIDNEY. Club's closed. There's a tart called Annabelle three
doors up, if that's what you want.

> *They look at each other and leave.*

Duncan. Harry. Tom.

BROWNE. Sidney . . .

> SIDNEY *ignores him.*

And Lucy. And the new Mr Lucy. Congratulations, Clive, just
what you always wanted. And Mum. (*Pause.*) Family conference. Party. (*Grandly.*) Dear . . . Octopus.

> MARTIN *walks on.*

Now we can start.

MARTIN. Where's father? I came to see father.

SIDNEY. Martin.

MARTIN. I've come all the way from Brussels, just to see father.
What have you done with him, Sidney?

LUCY. Father is heavily sedated. Dead to the world.

MARTIN. Sidney.

SIDNEY. In a hotel.

LUCY. In Hastings.

MARTIN. Sidney.

SIDNEY. We all picked him up at the gates of the Open Prison.
At nine o'clock this morning. And put him on a train.

MARTIN. What's wrong with him?

LUCY. He wants to live in a hut, in the countryside and grow
runner beans, and talk to the birds, and be dry and wiry.
(*Pause.*) We're all going to pay for a nurse.

MARTIN. I see.

SIDNEY. Nothing much happened while you've been away,
Martin. Being brilliant in Brussels, in your new career. At
your stainless steel desk. Speaking five languages.

MARTIN. Good job. Bon occupation.

SIDNEY. Does it ever embarrass you to remember your family,
Martin? Do your Eurocrat colleagues ever ask you if you are
related to that old fraud Bagley who got done in the English
Midlands?

MARTIN. I've changed my name. Martin is now my surname.

SIDNEY. Good. A much better name for a Eurocrat. What's
your christian name.

MARTIN. We don't use christian names much in Brussels.

CLIVE. Leave him alone, Sidney.

SIDNEY. Yes, you're right. Clear the decks. Start again. I have a
proposition, Martin. For the family. And its satellites. An
enterprise which demands we all play a part. A lush pasture.

Pause.

I have a proposition. There is a commodity, sold in occasional
market places, in these sad times, the world the way it is, a
product for our times, the perfect product, totally artificial,
man-made, creating its own market, one hundred percent con-
sumer identification, generating its own demand, if there's a
glut the demand goes up, if there's a famine the demand goes
up, an endless spiral of need and profit. Endless profit for all
human need is there. Gathering up all emotions in its moneyed
path. Hates and loves, jealousies and deceits. True, it kills. But
only in the end. So does washing up liquid and chocolate, in
the end. And my commodity thrives on dying. The dying and
the would-be dead are its market. It's a winner.

MARTIN. Chinese heroin.

SIDNEY. That's the stuff.

A long pause.

EDMUNDS. It's . . .

ROCHESTER. Well . . .

EDMUNDS. It's . . .

LUCY. Yes.

CLIVE. Well . . .

BASSETT. Oh aye . . .

BROWNE. Sidney.

EDMUNDS. 'Eroin, eh? (*He sniffs.*) Powder, in't it?

SIDNEY. Yes. Packets.

CLIVE. Yes.

SIDNEY. Like sherbet.

CLIVE. Yes.

SIDNEY. Grains. Like sand in your pocket.

EDMUNDS. Well . . .

SIDNEY. A pretty enviable product. The last product. The all-time merchandise. Better than parachutes. Better than bricks.

MARTIN. I can see why you want to go into it.

VANESSA. What does Sidney want, dear?

LUCY. He wants us to be heroin dealers, Mummy.

BROWNE. I was a communist in my youth. Now I'm looking for revenge. A revenge on everything I believed in. Count me in.

MARTIN. I can see why I want to go into it.

BASSETT. As a brewer I like to see people smashed out of their minds. Logical thing, greed.

CLIVE. I suppose if I felt anything at all I could think myself round to being disgusted.

MARTIN. I've always dreamt of something that will give me free and wild expression. Like Scott of the Antarctic.

VANESSA. I want to come alive again.

CLIVE. Luxurious disgust.

EDMUNDS. It's oozing. It's all beginning to ooze again.

LUCY. Terrific.

EDMUNDS. And I want to be there. My mouth open.
LUCY. Terrifically hard. And sexy. And money.
BROWNE. Sidney. Count me in.

ROCHESTER *leaps up.*

ROCHESTER. Look at me. Bill Rochester. Naked with greed. I
could take all my clothes off. Now. And greed would be
blazoned across my bum.
SIDNEY. Welcome, Bill. Leave your coat at the door. You're a
beautiful human being.

*The band strikes up. An extremely fast strip act begins. A girl
comes on wearing Mayor's robes. She starts stripping off.
Underneath she toys with Masonic aprons. Then strips down
to a bowler hat and away. This throughout the remainder of
the scene.*

A WAITER *distributes champagne.*

VANESSA. Poppies. It comes from poppies. A bleeding tender
flower.
MARTIN. Quality control?
SIDNEY. Marseilles laboratories.
CLIVE. Capital?
LUCY. Mum.
BASSETT. Delivery?
SIDNEY. Harry.
EDMUNDS. My 'and luggage.
BASSETT. Distribution?
SIDNEY. My girls.
CLIVE. Customers?
ROCHESTER. School kids.
LUCY. Overheads?
SIDNEY. Negligible.
BROWNE. Odd bribe.
LUCY. Profits?
SIDNEY. Name them. They're yours.

BROWNE (*singing over the band*). Greasy days are here again.
EDMUNDS. Expansion?
MARTIN. Worldwide.
SIDNEY. Infinite.
MARTIN. We could sell, eventually, to I.C.I.
BROWNE. Expertise?
SIDNEY. Us.
MARTIN. Us.

Round the stripper's middle is a rubber tube which she detaches and wraps round her upper arm.

BROWNE. We won't make the same mistakes again.
LUCY. Never go back.
ROCHESTER. Strip down.
CLIVE. Press on.
BASSETT. The market. My God, the market's unbelievable. Babes in prams.

He gestures a needle into his vein, excited.

VANESSA. It's so good to know what you want.

The naked STRIPPER fixes, then raises her hypodermic. Fanfare. End of strip. The curtains on the small stage close. The band stops playing. Stage lights to dazzling brightness.

SIDNEY. As head of a great English Family I give you all a toast. The last days of capitalism.

They lift their glasses in silence. The floor slowly gives way beneath them, and they descend as the lights fade and they are swallowed up.

Methuen's Modern Plays

Jean Anouilh	*Antigone*
	Becket
	The Lark
John Arden	*Serjeant Musgrave's Dance*
	The Workhouse Donkey
	Armstrong's Last Goodnight
John Arden and	*The Business of Good Government*
Margaretta D'Arcy	*The Royal Pardon*
	The Hero Rises Up
	The Island of the·Mighty
	Vandaleur's Folly
Wolfgang Bauer	*Shakespeare the Sadist*
Rainer Werner	
Fassbinder	*Bremen Coffee*
Peter Handke	*My Foot My Tutor*
Frank Xaver Kroetz	*Stallerhof*
Brendan Behan	*The Quare Fellow*
	The Hostage
	Richard's Cork Leg
Edward Bond	*A-A-America!* and *Stone*
	Saved
	Narrow Road to the Deep North
	The Pope's Wedding
	Lear
	The Sea
	Bingo
	The Fool and *We Come to the River*
	Theatre Poems and Songs
	The Bundle
	The Woman
	The Worlds with *The Activists Papers*
	Restoration and *The Cat*
	Summer and *Fables*
Bertolt Brecht	*Mother Courage and Her Children*
	The Caucasian Chalk Circle
	The Good Person of Szechwan
	The Life of Galileo

If you would like to receive, free of charge, regular information about new plays and theatre books from Methuen, please send your name and address to:

The Marketing Department (Drama)
Methuen London Ltd
North Way
Andover
Hampshire SP10 5BE